AIDS-related deaths in France

Table of Contents

Bernard-Marie Koltès 1
Bruce Chatwin 2
Copi 4
Cyril Collard 5
Daniel Bensaïd 5
Guy Hocquenghem 5
Hervé Guibert 7
Jacques Demy 7
Michel Foucault 8
Patrick Kelly (fashion designer) 19
Rémi Laurent 19
Rudolf Nureyev 19
Scott Ross (harpsichordist) 23
Serge Daney 24
Severo Sarduy 24
Thierry Le Luron 25
Thierry Paulin 26
Vincent Fourcade 27
Yves Mourousi 28
Yves Rault 28

Preface

Each chapter in this book ends with a URL to a hyperlinked online version. Use the online version to access related pages, websites, footnotes, tables, color photos, updates, or to see the chapter's contributors. Click the edit link to suggest changes. Please type the URL exactly as it appears. If you change the URL's capitalization, for example, it may not work.

Purchase of this book entitles you to a free trial membership in the publisher's book club at www.booksllc.net. (Time limited offer.) Simply enter the barcode number from the back cover onto the membership form on our home page. The book club entitles you to select from millions of books at no additional charge, including a digital copy of this and related books to read on the go. Simply enter the title or subject onto the search form to find them.

If you have any questions, could you please be so kind as to consult our Frequently Asked Questions page at www.booksllc.net/faqs.cfm? You are also welcome to contact us there.

Publisher: Books LLC, Wiki Series, Memphis, TN, USA, 2012.

Bernard-Marie Koltès

Bernard-Marie Koltès (9 April 1948, Metz – 15 April 1989, Paris) was a French playwright and director.

Life

Born in 1948 to a middle-class family in Metz, his life was violent and anchored in revolt. He tried his hand at writing at a very young age but later renounced it, and didn't take to the stage until the age of twenty. He garnered recognition for his work on a production of *Medea* (*Médée*) directed by Jorge Lavelli in 1970.

After seeing the film actress María Casares, he was inspired and resumed writing, completing around ten plays in his lifetime. His first piece, the long monologue, *The Night Just Before The Forests*, was staged in 1977 at the Avignon Festival, and subsequent productions were put on in collaboration with director Patrice Chéreau. Koltès died in 1989 due to complications from AIDS.

Writing

Koltès's work, based in real-life problems, expresses the tragedy of being alone and of death. His writing style accents the dramatic tension and the lyricism of his plays. Koltes is most famous for his plays *The Night Just Before the Forests* (*La Nuit juste avant les Forêts*, 1976), *Sallinger* (1977) and *In the Solitude of Cotton Fields* (*Dans la Solitude des Champs de Coton*, 1986). Many of these plays were first directed by Patrice Chéreau when he was artistic director of the Théâtre des Amandiers in Nanterre. Koltes also translated into French Shakespeare's *The Winter's Tale*.

It is evident that Genet and the absurdists influenced Koltès's writing. Like other absurdist writers, he felt exiled - in his case, as a homosexual in a heterosexual world. In Africa, he saw native cultures being wiped out by European influences. This theme brought forth *Black Battles with Dogs*. After a visit to America he wrote *Quay West* (1985), about a brother and sister in a foreign culture. The psychopathic killer Roberto Succo provided the inspiration for his final play *Roberto Zucco*. It was first performed posthumously in Berlin in 1990, directed by Peter Stein. It has since been performed across Europe and the United States.

Stagings

In spite of his particular poetry, Koltès's works have not been staged so much. In addition to Chereau, among world theatre directors we find:

Ivica Buljan
Jan Bosse
Frederic Dussenne
Doris Mirescu
Arthur Nauzyciel
Roberto Pacini
Jay Scheib
Giampiero Solari
Èric Vigner
Rachid Zanouda
Krzysztof Warlikowski
Julián Hernández

Plays

Bitterness (*Les Amertumes*) (1970)
La Marche (1970)
Heritage (*L'Héritage*) (1972)
Récits morts (1973)
Sallinger (1977)
The Night Just Before the Forests (*La Nuit juste avant les forêts*) (1977)
Black Battles with Dogs (*Combat de nègre et de chiens*) (1979)
Quay West (*Quai Ouest*) (1985)

In the Solitude of Cotton Fields (*Dans la solitude des champs de coton*) (1985)
Tabataba (1986)
Return to the Desert (*Retour au désert*) (1988)
Roberto Zucco (1988)

Source http://en.wikipedia.org/wiki/Bernard-Marie_Koltès

Bruce Chatwin

Bruce Chatwin
Born 13 May 1940 near Sheffield, England
Died 18 January 1989 (aged 48) Nice, France
Occupation Author, travel writer, art and architecture advisor
Nationality British (English)
Period 1977–89
Genres History, travel, fiction
Subjects Patagonia, slave trade, Britain, Europe, Australia, Afghanistan
Spouse(s) Elizabeth Chanler

Charles Bruce Chatwin (13 May 1940 – 18 January 1989) was an English novelist and travel writer. He won the James Tait Black Memorial Prize for his novel *On the Black Hill* (1982). Married and bisexual, he was one of the first prominent men in Britain known to have contracted HIV and died of AIDS, although he hid the facts of his illness.

Early life

Bruce Chatwin was born in 1940 in the Shearwood Road nursing home in Sheffield, England, and his first home was his grandparents' house in Dronfield, near Sheffield. His mother, Margharita (*née* Turnell), had moved back to her parents' home when Chatwin's father, Charles Chatwin, went away to serve with the Royal Naval Reserve. They had been living at Barnt Green, Worcestershire.

Chatwin spent his early childhood living with his parents in West Heath in Birmingham (then in Warwickshire), where his father had a law practice. He was educated at Marlborough College, in Wiltshire.

Art and archaeology

After leaving Marlborough in 1958, Chatwin reluctantly moved to London to work as a porter in the Works of Art department at the auction house Sotheby's. Thanks to his sharp visual acuity, he quickly became Sotheby's expert on Impressionist art. He later became a director of the company.

In late 1964 he began to suffer from problems with his sight, which he attributed to the close analysis of artwork entailed by his job. He consulted eye specialist Patrick Trevor-Roper, who diagnosed a latent squint and recommended that Chatwin take a six-month break from his work at Sotheby's. Trevor-Roper had been involved in the design of an eye hospital in Addis Ababa, and suggested Chatwin visit east Africa. In February 1965, Chatwin left for the Sudan. On his return, Chatwin quickly became disenchanted with the art world, and turned his interest to archaeology. He resigned from his Sotheby's post in the early summer of 1966.

Chatwin enrolled at the University of Edinburgh to study archaeology in October, 1966. Despite winning the Wardrop Prize for the best first year's work, he found the rigour of academic archaeology tiresome. He spent only two years there and left without taking a degree.

Literary career

The southern part of the Grwyne Fechan valley in the Black Mountains

In 1972, Chatwin was hired by the *Sunday Times Magazine* as an adviser on art and architecture. His association with the magazine cultivated his narrative skills. Chatwin travelled on many international assignments, writing on such subjects as Algerian migrant workers and the Great Wall of China, and interviewing such diverse people as André Malraux in France, and the author Nadezhda Mandelstam in the Soviet Union.

In 1972, Chatwin interviewed the 93-year-old architect and designer Eileen Gray in her Paris salon, where he noticed a map of the area of South America called Patagonia, which she had painted. "I've always wanted to go there," Bruce told her. "So have I," she replied, "go there for me." Two years later in November 1974, Chatwin flew out to Lima in Peru, and reached Patagonia a month later. When he arrived, he left the newspaper with a telegram: "Have gone to Patagonia." He spent six months in the area, a trip which resulted in the book *In Patagonia* (1977). This work established his reputation as a travel writer. Later, however, residents in the region contradicted the account of events depicted in Chatwin's book. It was the first, but not the last time in his career, that conversations and characters which Chatwin presented as fact were alleged to have been fictionalised.

Later works included a novel based on the slave trade, *The Viceroy of Ouidah,* which he researched with extended stays in Benin, West Africa. For *The Songlines* (1987), a work combining fiction and non-fiction, Chatwin went to Australia. He studied the culture to express how the songs of the Aborigines are a cross between a creation myth, an atlas and an Aboriginal man's personal story. He also related the travelling expressed in *The Songlines* to his own travels and the long nomadic past of humans.

Winner of the James Tait Black Memorial Prize, his novel *On the Black*

Hill (1982) was set closer to home, in the hill farms of the Welsh Borders. It focuses on the relationship between twin brothers, Lewis and Benjamin, who grow up isolated from the course of twentieth century history. *Utz* (1988), was a novel about the obsession that leads people to collect. Set in Prague, the novel details the life and death of Kaspar Utz, a man obsessed with his collection of Meissen porcelain. Chatwin was working on a number of new ideas for future novels at the time of his death in 1989, including a transcontinental epic, provisionally titled *Lydia Livingstone*.

Style and influence

Chatwin is admired for his spare, lapidary style and his innate story-telling abilities. However, he has also been criticised for his fictionalised anecdotes of real people, places, and events. Frequently, the people he wrote about recognised themselves and did not always appreciate his distortions of their culture and behaviour. Chatwin was philosophical about what he saw as an unavoidable dilemma, arguing that his portrayals were not intended to be faithful representations. As his biographer Nicholas Shakespeare argues: "He tells not a half truth, but a truth and a half."

Personal life

Much to the surprise of many of his friends, Chatwin married Elizabeth Chanler (a descendant of John Jacob Astor) on 26 August 1965. He had met Chanler at Sotheby's, where she worked as a secretary. Chatwin was bisexual throughout his married life, a circumstance his wife knew and accepted. They had no children. After fifteen years of marriage, she asked for a separation and sold their farmhouse at Ozleworth in Gloucestershire. Toward the end of his life, they reconciled. According to Chatwin's biographer Nicholas Shakespeare, the Chatwins' marriage seems to have been celibate. He describes Chatwin as homosexual rather than bisexual.

Chatwin was known as a socialite in addition to being a recognised travel author. His circle of friends extended far and wide. He was renowned for accepting hospitality and patronage from a powerful set of friends and allies. Penelope Betjeman – wife of the poet laureate John Betjeman – showed him the border country of Wales. She helped in the gestation of the book that would become *On the Black Hill*. Tom Maschler, the publisher, was also a patron to Chatwin during this time, lending him his house in the area as a writing retreat. Later, Chatwin visited Patrick Leigh Fermor in his house near Kardamyli, in the Peloponnese of Greece. Numbered among his lovers was Jasper Conran.

He extensively used moleskines, a particular style of notebooks manufactured in France. When production stopped in 1986, he bought up the entire supply at his stationery store.

German filmmaker Werner Herzog relates a story about meeting Chatwin in Australia while Herzog was working on his 1984 film, *Where the Green Ants Dream*. Finding out that Chatwin was in Australia researching a book (*The Songlines*), Herzog sought him out. Herzog states that Chatwin professed his admiration for him, and when they met was carrying one of Herzog's books, *On Walking In Ice*. The two hit it off immediately, united by a shared love of adventure and telling tall tales. Herzog states that he and Chatwin talked almost nonstop over two days, telling each other stories. He said that Chatwin "told about three times as many as me." Herzog also claims that when Chatwin was near death, he gave Herzog his leather rucksack and said,"You're the one who has to wear it now, you're the one who's walking."

In 1987, Herzog made *Cobra Verde*, a film based on Chatwin's 1980 novel *The Viceroy of Ouidah*, depicting the life of Francisco Manoel da Silva, a fictional Brazilian slave trader working in West Africa. Locations for the film included Brazil, Colombia and Ghana.

Death

Around 1980, Chatwin contracted HIV. Chatwin told different stories about how he contracted the virus, such as that he was gang-raped in Dahomey, and that he believed he caught the disease from Sam Wagstaff, the patron and lover of photographer Robert Mapplethorpe. He was one of the first high-profile people in Britain to have the disease. Although he hid the illness – passing off his symptoms as fungal infections or the effects of the bite of a Chinese bat, a typically exotic cover story – it was a poorly kept secret. He did not respond well to AZT, and suffered increasing bouts of psychosis. With his condition deteriorating rapidly, Chatwin and his wife went to live in the South of France at the house belonging to Shirley Conran, the mother of his one-time lover, Jasper Conran. There, during his final months, Chatwin was nursed by both his wife and Shirley Conran. He died in Nice in 1989 at age 48.

A memorial service was held in the Greek Orthodox Church of Saint Sophia in West London. It happened to be the same day that a *fatwa* was announced on Salman Rushdie, a close friend of Chatwin's who attended the service. Paul Theroux, a one-time friend who also attended the service, later commented on it and Chatwin in a piece for *Granta*. The novelist Martin Amis described the memorial service in the essay "Salman Rushdie", included in his anthology *Visiting Mrs. Nabokov*.

Chatwin's ashes were scattered near a Byzantine chapel above Kardamyli in the Peloponnese. This was close to the home of one of his mentors, the writer Patrick Leigh Fermor.

Works

In Patagonia (1977)
The Viceroy of Ouidah (1980)
On the Black Hill (1982)
The Songlines (1987)
Utz (1988)
What Am I Doing Here (1988)
Photographs and Notebooks (1993)
Anatomy of Restlessness (1997)
Winding Paths (1998)
Source http://en.wikipedia.org/wiki/Bruce_Chatwin

Copi

Raúl Damonte Botana (November 20, 1939, Buenos Aires – December 14, 1987, Paris), better known by the nom de plume **Copi** (for "copito de nieve", Spanish for "little snowflake"), was an Argentine writer, cartoonist, and playwright who spent most of his career in Paris.

Biography

Damonte spent most of his youth in Montevideo. His maternal grandfather was the journalist Natalio Félix Botana and his father was the journalist Raúl Damonte Taborda, an antiperonist Radical politician and director of the journal *Tribuna Popular*. Raúl showed an early talent for drawing and, from his adolescence, contributed caricatures to his father's publication and to the satirical magazine *Tía Vicenta*.

His father's political activities forced the family into exile in Uruguay, Haiti, and later New York. He finally settled in Paris, where he embarked on a career as a cartoonist for such newspapers as Le Nouvel Observateur. His most notable character during this period was *La Femme assise*, The Sitting Woman.

He was a member of *Tse*, an association of Franco-Argentine artists with whom in 1969 he staged a biographical play about Eva Perón. His theatrical works, influenced by Samuel Beckett, are characterized by the failure of characters to communicate.

Copi also collaborated with the avant-garde group *Pánico*, which included Fernando Arrabal, Roland Topor, and Alejandro Jodorowsky.

Copi contributed cartoons to the magazine Gai Pied.

He died of an AIDS-related illness in 1987, at the age of 48.

The Argentine writer César Aira, who wrote an essay on Copi, has given lectures on his works in the Ricardo Rojas Cultural Center and is credited with popularizing Copi in Argentina. His posthumous reputation is based largely on his plays, stories, and novels.

Novels

L'Uruguayen, Christian Bourgois, 1973
Le bal des folles, Christian Bourgois, 1977
Une langouste pour deux, Christian Bourgois, 1978
La cité des rats, Belfond, 1979
La vida es un tango, Anagrama, 1981(his only finished novel in Spanish)
La guerre des pédés, Albin Michel, 1982 (written in Spanish but unedited)
Virginia Woolf a encore frappé, Persona, 1983
L'Internationale argentine, Belfond, 1988

Theater

Un ángel para la señora Lisca, Buenos Aires, directed by Copi, 1962.
Sainte Geneviève dans sa baignoire, Le Bilboquet, directed by Jorge Lavelli, 1966.
L'alligator, le thé, International festival of UNEF, directed by Jérome Savary, 1966.
La journée d'une rêveuse, Theater of Lutèce, directed by Jorge Lavelli, 1968.
Eva Perón, Theater of l'Épée-de-Bois, directed by Alfredo Arias, 1970.
L'homosexuel ou la difficulté de s'exprimer, City University Theater, directed by Jorge Lavelli, 1971. Spanish title: *El homosexual, o la dificultad de expresarse*.
Les quatre jumelles, Le Palace, directed by Jorge Lavelli, 1973.
Loretta Strong, Theater of the Gaïté Montparnasse, directed by Javier Botana, 1974.
La Pyramide, Le Palace, directed by Copi, 1975.
La coupe du monde, Le Sélénite, directed by Copi, 1975.
L'ombre de Venceslao, Festival de la Rochelle, directed by Jérome Savary, 1978.
La Tour de la Défense, Teatro Fontaine, directed by Claude Confortès, 1981.
Le Frigo, Fontaine Theater, 1983.
La nuit de Madame Lucienne, Avignon Festival, directed by Jorge Lavelli, 1985.
Une visite inopportune, Théâtre de la Colline, directed by Jorge Lavelli, 1988.
Les escaliers du Sacré-cœur, Aubervilliers Theater, directed by Alfredo Arias, 1990.
Une visite inopportune Konex Theatre Buenos Aires,directed by Stephan Druet with Moria Casan,2009

Comics

Le dernier salon où l'on cause, Ediciones de Square.
Et moi, pourquoi j'ai pas de banane?, Ediciones de Square, 1975.
Les vieilles putes, Editions du Square, 1977. Italian title: *Storie puttanesche*, Mondadori, Milan 1979.
Le monde fantastique des gays 1986. Italian title: *Il fantastico mondo dei gay... e delle loro mamme!*, Glénat Italia, Milan 1987.
La femme assise, Stock, 2002.
Un livre blanc, Buchet-Castel, 2002. Italian title: *Un libro bianco*.
Les poulets n'ont pas de chaises. Italian title: *I polli non hanno sedie*, Glénat Italia, 1988. ISBN 88-7811-015-9.

Opera

Les quatre jumelles, composed by Régis Campo, premièred in Nanterre, France, Jan. 2009
Cachafaz, composed by Oscar Strasnoy, premièred in Quimper, France, Nov. 2010

Other

Copi, collected works edited by Jorge Damonte and Christian Bourgois, 1990.
Source http://en.wikipedia.org/wiki/Copi

Cyril Collard

This article is about the French author, filmmaker, composer and actor. For the Australian footballer see Cyril Collard (footballer).

Cyril Collard (19 December 1957, Paris – 5 March 1993) was a French author, filmmaker, composer, musician and actor. He is known for his unapologetic portrayals of bisexuality and HIV in art, particularly his autobiographical novel and film *Les Nuits Fauves* (*Savage Nights*). Openly bisexual, Collard was also one of the first French artists to speak openly about his HIV-positive status.

Early life

Collard was born into a liberal, middle-class family in France. He attended Lycée Hoche in Versailles, and pursued an engineering degree at Institut Industriel du Nord in Villeneuve d'Ascq, later known as École centrale de Lille before deciding to drop out.

Source http://en.wikipedia.org/wiki/Cyril_Collard

Daniel Bensaïd

Bensaïd at a conference in Barcelona in April 2008

Born March 25, 1946
Toulouse
Died January 12, 2010 (aged 63)
Paris
Era 20th century philosophy
Region Western philosophy
School Trotskyism

Daniel Bensaïd (25 March 1946 – 12 January 2010) was a philosopher and a leader of the Trotskyist movement in France. He became a leading figure in the student revolt of 1968, while studying at the University of Paris X: Nanterre.

Life and career

Bensaïd was born in Toulouse, to a father who was a Sephardic Jew from Algeria, and who had moved from Oran, where he met Bensaïd's mother, to Vichy Toulouse. In response to the 8 February 1962 Charonne massacre of Algerians in Paris, Bensaïd joined the Union of Communist Students. Irritated by the party orthodoxy he swiftly became part of a left opposition within the union, and was among the dissidents expelled from the party in 1966.

In 1966 Bensaïd began studying at the École normale supérieure de Saint-Cloud, where he helped found the *Jeunesse Communiste Révolutionnaire*, which became the Ligue Communiste Révolutionnaire (LCR). With Daniel Cohn-Bendit he helped to found the Mouvement du 22 Mars (Movement of 22 March) which was involved in the protests of May 1968 in France.

He became a leading theorist of the LCR and the United Secretariat of the Fourth International, and a professor of philosophy at the University of Paris-VIII. He was also a Fellow at the International Institute for Research and Education. Upon his death, Tariq Ali described him as "France's leading Marxist public intellectual, much in demand on talkshows and writing essays and reviews in *Le Monde* and *Libération*." He was known for his studies of Walter Benjamin and Karl Marx, and a recent analysis of French postmodernism.

He died of cancer arising from the side effects of drugs used to treat AIDS, which he had had for the previous 16 years.

Criticism and debate

Bensaïd and the Fourth International tradition have come under attack from sections of the far left for the strategy they have advanced in the social movements; in particular, for seeing reform and revolution as a false dichotomy, and proposing the formation of "broad parties". In one such critique, Luke Cooper criticised Bensaïd for arguing that—in certain, specific circumstances—it maybe permissible to enter a capitalist government, and seek to use the existing state as an instrument of revolutionary transformation. Bensaïd also debated revolutionary strategy with other Fourth International members, and the British Socialist Workers Party's Alex Callinicos.

Source http://en.wikipedia.org/wiki/Daniel_Bensaïd

Guy Hocquenghem

Born 3 December 1946
Paris, France
Died 28 August 1988 (aged 42)
Paris, France
Era 20th-century philosophy
Region Western Philosophy
School Continental philosophy, Queer theory

Guy Hocquenghem (3 December 1946

– 28 August 1988) was a French writer and queer theorist.

Biography

Guy Hocquenghem was born in the suburbs of Paris and was educated at the Lycée Lakanal in Sceaux and the Ecole Normale Supérieure in Paris. At the age of fifteen he began an affair with his high school philosophy teacher, René Scherer. They remained lifelong friends. His participation in the May 1968 student rebellion in France formed his allegiance to the Communist Party, which later expelled him because of his homosexuality.

Hocquenghem taught philosophy at the University of Vincennes-Saint Denis, Paris and wrote numerous novels and works of theory. He was the staff writer for the French publication *Libération*. Hocquenghem was the first gay man to be a member of the Front Homosexuel d'Action Révolutionnaire (FHAR), originally formed by lesbian separatists who split from the Mouvement Homophile de France in 1971. With filmmaker Lionel Soukaz (b. 1953), Hocquenghem wrote and produced a documentary film about gay history, *Race d'Ep!* (1979) the last word of the title being a play on the word *pédé*, a French slur for gay men.

Though Hocquenghem had a significant impact on leftist thinking in France, his reputation has failed to grow to international prominence. Only the first of his theoretical tracts, *Homosexual Desire* (1972) and his first novel, *L'Amour en relief* (1982) have been translated into English. Although *Race d'Ep!* was shown at Roxie Cinema in San Francisco in April 1980 and released in America as *The Homosexual Century*, like Hocquenghem, the film is virtually unknown.

Career

Guy Hocquenghem's *Homosexual Desire* (1972, English translation 1978) may be the first work of Queer Theory. Drawing on the theories of desiring-production developed by Gilles Deleuze and Félix Guattari in their *Capitalism and Schizophrenia* project (1972-1980), Hocquenghem critiqued the influential models of the psyche and sexual desire derived from Lacan and Freud. The author also addressed the relation of capitalism to sexualities, the dynamics of desire, and the political effects of gay group-identities. Moreover, he repudiated the prospect of a new gay 'social organisation' of politics, along with the injunction to sacrifice oneself in the name of future generations.

Jeffrey Weeks's 1978 preface to the first English language translation of *Homosexual Desire* situates the essay in relation to the various, mostly French, theories of subjectivity and desire surrounding and influencing Hocquenghem's thought. It was republished in French in 2000.

L'Après-Mai des faunes (1974) is the second and untranslated queer-theoretical text.

Co-ire, album systématique de l'enfance (*Co-anger: systematic album of childhood*) (1976) examines childhood sexuality from a Marxist perspective, co-written with professor René Schérer. It is rumored that Schérer and Hocquenghem had an affair in 1959, when the latter was 15.

Fin de section (1976) short story collection

La Dérive homosexuelle (1977) is the third and yet to be translated queer-theoretical text.

La Beauté du métis (1979) analyzed French anti-Arab feeling and homophobia.

L'Amour en relief (1982) is Hocquenghem's first and most famous novel. A blind Tunisian boy explores French society and discovers the ways in which pleasure can form a resistance to totalitarianism. The novel gives context to homosexual desire as a resistance to white supremacy and racism.

La Colère de l'agneau (*The Wrath of the Lamb*) (1985) is an experiment in millenarian and apocoliptic narrative taking St. John the Evangelist as its subject.

L'Âme atomique (*The Atomic Heart*) (1986) was written partly as a response to his deteriorating health, and again in collaboration with Schérer, this work espouses a philosophy composed of dandyism, gnosticism, and epicureanism.

Open letter to those who moved from Mao collars to Rotary wheels, Marseilles, Agone (1986) was republished in 2003 with a foreword by Serge Halimi ISBN 2-7489-0005-7

Eve (1987) is a narrative which combines the story of Genesis with the description of the changes in the body from AIDS-related symptoms and written as Hocquenghem's own body deteriorated.

Voyages et aventures extraordinaires du Frère Angelo (1988) explores the mind of an Italian monk accompanying the conquistadors to the New World.

Death

Hocquenghem died of AIDS on 28 August 1988, age 41.

Works

Homosexual Desire (1972, English translation 1978)
L'Après-Mai des faunes (1974)
Co-ire, album systématique de l'enfance (*Co-anger: systematic album of childhood*, with René Schérer) (1976)
Fin de section (1976) short stories
La Dérive homosexuelle (1977)
La Beauté du métis (1979)
Gay Travels: guide and glance homosexual over the large metropolises (1980)
L'Amour en relief (1982)
La Colère d'agneau (*The Wrath of the Lamb*) (1985)
L'Âme atomique (*The Atomic Heart*, with René Schérer) (1986)
Open letter to those who moved from Mao Collars to Rotary Wheels (1986)
Eve (1987)
(in French) *Les voyages et aventures extraordinaires du frère Angelo*, Le Livre de Poche, A. Michel, 1988, ISBN 978-2-226-03442-7
The amphitheatre of the dead ones: anticipated memories (1994)

Works on Hocquenghem

Bill Marshall, *Guy Hocquenghem: Gay Beyond Identity* (Duke University Press, 1996)

Source http://en.wikipedia.org/wiki/Guy_Hocquenghem

Hervé Guibert

Hervé Guibert (14 December 1955 - 27 December 1991) was a French writer and photographer. The author of numerous novels and autobiographical studies, he played a considerable role in changing French public attitudes to AIDS. He was a close friend of Michel Foucault.

Early life and career

Guibert was born in Saint-Cloud, Hauts-de-Seine, to a middle-class family and spent his early years in Paris, moving to La Rochelle from 1970 to 1973. After working as a filmmaker and actor, he turned to photography and journalism. In 1978, he successfully applied for a job at France's prestigious evening paper *Le Monde* and published his second book, *Les aventures singulières* (published by Éditions de minuit). In 1984, Guibert shared a César Award for best screenplay with Patrice Chéreau for *L'homme blessé*. Guibert had met Chéreau in the 1970s during his theatrical years.

Guibert's writing style was inspired by the French writer Jean Genet. Three of his lovers occupied an important place in his life and work: Thierry Jouno, director of an institute for the blind whom he met in 1976, and which led to his novel *Des aveugles*; Michel Foucault, whom he met in 1977; and Vincent M., a teenager of fifteen who inspired his novel *Fou de Vincent*.

In January 1988 Guibert was diagnosed with AIDS. From then on, he worked at recording what was left of his life. In June the following year, he married Christine, the partner of Thierry Jouno, so that his royalty income would eventually pass to her and her two children. In 1990, Guibert publicly revealed his HIV status in his roman à clef *À l'ami qui ne m'a pas sauvé la vie* (published in English as *To the Friend Who Did Not Save My Life*). Guibert immediately found himself the focus of media attention, featured in newspapers and appearing on several television talk shows.

Two more books also detailing the progress of his illness followed: *Le Protocole compassionnel* (published in English as *The Compassionate Protocol*) and *L'Homme au chapeau rouge* (published in English as *The Man In The Red Hat*), which was released posthumously in January 1992, the same month French television screened *La Pudeur ou l'impudeur*, a home-made film by Guibert of his last year as he lost his battle against AIDS. Almost blind as a result of disease, he attempted to end his life just before his 36th birthday, and died two weeks later.

Source http://en.wikipedia.org/wiki/Hervé_Guibert

Jacques Demy

Jacques Demy

Born	5 June 1931 Pontchâteau, Loire-Atlantiq Pays-de-la-Loire, France
Died	27 October 1990 (aged 59) Paris, Île-de-France, France
Years active	1955–88
Spouse(s)	Agnès Varda (1962–90)

Jacques Demy (5 June 1931 – 27 October 1990) was one of the most approachable filmmakers to appear in the wake of the French New Wave. Uninterested in the formal experimentation of Alain Resnais, or the political agitation of Jean-Luc Godard, Demy instead created a self-contained fantasy world closer to that of François Truffaut, drawing on musicals, fairytales and the golden age of Hollywood.

Career

After working with the animator Paul Grimault and the filmmaker Georges Rouquier, Demy directed his first feature film, *Lola*, in 1961, with Anouk Aimée playing the eponymous cabaret singer. The Demy universe here emerges full-fledged. Characters burst into song (courtesy of composer and lifelong Demy-collaborator Michel Legrand); iconic Hollywood imagery is lovingly appropriated as in the opening scene with the man in a white Stetson in the Cadillac, daringly set to Beethoven's "Seventh Symphony"); plot is dictated by the director's fascination with fate, and stock themes of chance encounters and long-lost love; and the setting, as with so many of Demy's films, is the French Atlantic coast of his childhood, specifically the seaport town of Nantes.

La Baie des Anges (*The Bay of Angels*, 1963), starring Jeanne Moreau, took the theme of fate further, with its story of love at the roulette tables.

Demy is best known for his original musical, *Les Parapluies de Cherbourg* (*The Umbrellas of Cherbourg*, 1964), with a score by Legrand. Although the subversion of established genres was a typically New Wave obsession (notably Godard's playful thriller-cum-sci-fi, *Alphaville*), Demy was unusual in actually recreating them literally. The whimsical concept of singing all the dialogue sets the tone for this tragedy of the everyday. The film also sees the emergence of Demy's trademark visual style: whereas *Lola*, filmed by Godard's cinematographer Raoul Coutard, has a New Wave black and white austerity, *Les Parapluies* is shot in saturated supercolour, with every detail — neck-ties, wallpaper, even Catherine Deneuve's bleached-blonde hair — selected for maximum visual impact. Interestingly, the young man, Roland Cassard, from *Lola* (Marc Michel) reappears here, marrying Deneuve. Such reappearances are typical of Demy's work.

Demy's subsequent films never quite captured audience and critical acclaim the way that "Les Parapluies" had, although he continued to make ambitious and original dramas and musicals. *Les Demoiselles de Rochefort* (1967), another whimsical musical, features Deneuve and her real-life sister Françoise Dorléac as sisters living in the seaside town of Rochefort, daughters of Danielle Darrieux. It has stunning color photography, some of the best French songs of the period (it was nominated for an Oscar for best musical score), and breathtaking dancing by Gene Kelly and West Side Story's George Chakiris. Lola reappears in the naturalistic drama Model Shop (1969), his first American film, starring Gary Lockwood as a confused young architect navigating the streets of Los Angeles looking for love and meaning in life. *Peau d'Âne* (*Donkey Skin*, 1970) is a visually extravagant musical interpretation of a classic French fairytale which highlights the tale's incestuous overtones, starring Deneuve, Jean Marais, and Delphine Seyrig.

Subsequent films are less highly regarded, but may well be due for reappraisal: David Thomson wrote about "the fascinating application of the operatic technique to an unusually dark story" in *Une chambre en ville* (*A Room in Town*, 1982). *L'événement le plus important depuis que l'homme a marché sur la lune (1973)* ("A Slightly Pregnant Man") is an interesting look back at the pressures of second-wave feminism in France, and the fears it elicited in men. After years of neglect, Demy's strengths have been recognized, and *Parapluies de Cherbourg* was digitally restored and reissued to great acclaim in 1998.

Demy was the husband of fellow director Agnès Varda, whose *Jacquot de Nantes*, a film version of Demy's autobiographical notebooks, is a loving account of Demy's childhood and his lifelong love of theatre and cinema. Demy himself appears in the film in the opening and closing sequences, and at several points throughout.

Jacques Demy died of AIDS (information given in Agnès Varda's 2008 autobiographical movie *Les Plages d'Agnès*) in 1990 at age 59 and was interred in the Montparnasse Cemetery in Montparnasse.

Select filmography

Ars (1959)
Lola (1960)
La Luxure, episode in *Les Sept péchés capitaux* (1961)
La Baie des Anges (1962)
Les Parapluies de Cherbourg (1964)
Les Demoiselles de Rochefort (1967)
Model Shop (1969)
Peau d'Âne (*The Donkey Skin* or *The Magic Donkey*) (1970)
The Pied Piper (1972)
L'événement le plus important depuis que l'homme a marché sur la lune (*The slightly pregnant man*) (1973)
Lady Oscar (1979)
La Naissance du Jour (made for TV, 1979)
Une chambre en ville ("A room in town") (1982)
Parking (1982)
La table tournante (1988)
Trois places pour le 26 (1988)
Source http://en.wikipedia.org/wiki/Jacques_Demy

Michel Foucault

Born	15 October 1926 Poitiers, France
Died	25 June 1984 (aged 57 Paris, France
Era	20th century philosoph
Region	Western philosophy
School	Continental philosoph structuralism, discours
Main interests	History of ideas, epist ethics, political philos losophy of literature
Notable ideas	"Archaeology", biopov plinary institution, *dis*, *épistémè*, "Genealogy" mentality, power-knov panopticism

Michel Foucault (French: [miʃɛl fuko]; born **Paul-Michel Foucault**) (15 October 1926 – 25 June 1984) was a French philosopher, social theorist, historian of ideas, and literary critic. He held a chair at the Collège de France with the title "History of Systems of Thought", and lectured at both the University at Buffalo and the University of California, Berkeley. His philosophical theories addressed what power is and how it works, the manner in which it controls knowledge and vice versa, and how it is used as a form of social control.

Born into a middle class family in Poitiers, Foucault was educated at the Lycée Henri-IV and then the École Normale Supérieure, where he developed a keen interest in philosophy and came under the influence of his tutors Jean Hyppolite and Louis Althusser. After several years as a cultural diplomat abroad, he returned to France and published his first major book, *Madness and Civilization* (1961), which explored the history of the mental institution in Europe. After obtaining work between 1960 and 1966 at the University of Clermont-Ferrand, he produced two more significant publications, *The Birth of the Clinic* (1963) and *The Order of Things* (1966), which displayed his increasing involvement with structuralism, a theoretical movement in social anthropology from which he later distanced himself.

From 1966 to 1968 he lectured at the University of Tunis, Tunisia before returning to France, where he involved himself in several protest movements and associated with far left groups. He then proceeded to publish on the history of prison systems. His final work was the three-volume *The History of Sexuality*. Foucault died in Paris of neurological problems compounded by the HIV/AIDS virus; he was the first famous figure in France to have died from the virus, with his partner Daniel Defert founding the AIDES charity in his memory.

He also rejected the poststructuralist and postmodernist labels later attributed to him, preferring to classify his thought as a critical history of modernity. Foucault is best known for his critical studies of social institutions, most notably psychiatry, social anthropology of medicine, the human sciences, and the prison system, as well as for his work on the history of human sexuality. His writings on power, knowledge, and discourse have been widely influential in academic circles. His project was particularly influenced by Nietzsche, his "genealogy of knowledge" being a direct allusion to Nietzsche's "genealogy of morality". In an interview he stated: "I am a Nietzschean."

Biography

Childhood: 1926–1946

Paul-Michel Foucault was born on 15 October 1926 in the small town of Poitiers, west-central France, as the second of three children to a prosperous and socially conservative upper-middle-class family. He had been named after his father, Dr. Paul Foucault, as was the family tradition, but his mother insisted on the addition of the double-barrelled "Michel"; while he would always be referred to as "Paul" at school, throughout his life he always expressed a preference for "Michel". His father (1893–1959) was a successful local surgeon, having been born in Fontainebleau before moving to Poitiers, where he set up his own practice and married local woman Anne Malapert. She was the daughter of prosperous surgeon Dr. Prosper Malapert, who owned a private practice in Poitiers and taught anatomy at the University of Poitiers' School of Medicine. Paul Foucault eventually took over his father-in-law's medical practice as well, while his wife took charge of their large mid-19th century house, Le Piroir, located at the village of Vendeuvre-du-Poitou 15 kilometres from the town. Together the couple had 3 children, a girl named Francine and two boys, Paul-Michel and Denys, all of whom shared the same fair hair and bright blue eyes. These children were raised to be nominal Roman Catholics, attending mass at the Church of Saint-Porchair, and while Michel briefly became an altar boy, none of the family were particularly devout.

— Michel Foucault, 1983.

In later life, Foucault would reveal very little about his childhood. Describing himself as a "juvenile delinquent", he noted that his father was a "bully" who would sternly punish him for his misbehaviour. In 1930, Foucault began his schooling at the local Lycée Henry-IV despite the fact that he was two years younger than the usual entrance age of six. Here he would undertake two years of elementary education before entering the main *lycée*, where he stayed until 1936. He then undertook his first four years of secondary education at the same establishment, excelling in French, Greek, Latin and history but doing poorly at mathematics. In 1939, the Second World War broke out and France was occupied by the armies of Nazi Germany until 1945; his parents opposed the occupation and the Vichy regime who collaborated with them, but did not join the French Resistance. In 1940, Foucault's mother took him from his previous school and enrolled him in the Collège Saint-Stanislas, a strict Roman Catholic institution run by the Jesuits; here, he remained lonely, with few friends. Describing his years there as the "ordeal", he nevertheless excelled academically, particularly in the fields of philosophy, history and literature. In 1942, he entered his final year, the *terminale*, where he focused on the study of philosophy, earning his *baccalauréat* in 1943. That year, he then returned to the local Lycée Henry-IV, where he studied history and philosophy for a year. During this period, Foucault was aided in his studies by a personal tutor, the philosopher Louis Girard.

Rejecting his father's wishes that he become a surgeon, in 1945 Foucault traveled to the French capital of Paris, where he enrolled in one of the country's most prestigious secondary schools, which was also known as the Lycée Henri-IV. Here, he briefly studied under the philosopher Jean Hyppolite (1907–1968), an existentialist and expert on the work of 19th century German philosopher Georg Wilhelm Friedrich Hegel (1770–1831). Hyppolite devoted his energies to uniting the existentialist theories then in vogue among French philosophers with the dialectical theories of Hegel and Karl Marx (1818–1883); these ideas influenced the young Foucault, who would adopt Hyppolite's conviction that philosophy must be developed through a study of history. As a result, in ensuing years he would defend those who proposed a Marxist interpretation of history coupled with the existentialist view of the human individual.

École Normale Supérieure: 1946–1951

Attaining excellent results at the school, in the autumn of 1946 Foucault was admitted to the elite École Normale Supérieure (ENS); in order to get in, he had to undertake a series of exams and oral interrogation by Georges Canguilhem and Pierre-Maxime Schuhl. Of the hundred students entering the ENS, Foucault was ranked fourth based on his entry results, and encountered the highly competitive nature of the institution. Like most of his classmates, he was housed in the school's communal dormitories, located on the Parisian Rue d'Ulm. He remained largely unpopular among the other students, and spent much of his time alone, reading voraciously. His fellow students noted him for his love of violence and the macabre; he had decorated his bedroom with the images of torture and war drawn during the Napoleonic Wars by Spanish artist Francisco Goya (1746–1828), and on one occasion chased one of his classmates while brandishing a dagger. Prone to self-harm, in 1948 Foucault allegedly undertook a failed suicide attempt, for which his father sent him to see the psychiatrist Jean Delay (1907–1987) at the Hôpital Sainte-Anne. Obsessed with the idea of self-mutilation and suicide, Foucault would attempt the latter several times in ensuing years, and praised the act of killing oneself in a number of his later writings. The École Normale Supérieure's doctor examined Foucault's state of mind, suggesting that his suicidal tendencies emerged from the distress surrounding his homosexuality, which was then legal but socially taboo in France. At the time, Foucault engaged in homosexual activity with men whom he encountered in the underground Parisian gay scene, also indulging in drug use; according to biographer James Miller, he particularly enjoyed the thrill and sense of danger that these activities offered him.

Although studying an array of subjects at the school, Foucault's particular interest was soon drawn to philosophy, reading not only the works of Hegel and Marx that he had been exposed to by Hyppolite but also studying the writings of the philosophers Immanuel Kant (1724–1804), Edmund Husserl (1859–1938) and most significantly, Martin Heidegger (1889–1976). He also began to read the publications of philosopher Gaston Bachelard (1884–1962), taking a particular interest in his work exploring the history of science. In 1948, the philosopher Louis Althusser (1918–1980) became a tutor at the École Normale Supérieure. A Marxist, he proved to be an influence both on Foucault and a number of other students, encouraging them to join the French Communist Party (*Parti communiste français* - PCF), which Foucault duly did in 1950. Despite this, he never became particularly active in any of its activities, and never adopted an orthodox Marxist viewpoint, refuting concepts such as class struggle which were central to Marxist thought. He would soon become dissatisfied with the bigotry that he experienced within the party's ranks; he personally faced homophobia and was also appalled by the anti-semitism exhibited in the Doctors' plot that occurred in the Soviet Union. He left the Communist Party in 1953, but would remain a friend and defender of Althusser for the rest of his life. Although failing at the first attempt in 1950, he passed his *agrégation* in philosophy on the second try, in 1951. Excused from national service on medical grounds, he decided that he wanted to go on and study for a doctorate at the Fondation Thiers, focusing in on the philosophy of psychology.

Early career: 1951–1955

In the early 1950s, Foucault came under the influence of German philosopher Friedrich Nietzsche, who would remain a core influence on his work throughout his life.

Over the following few years, Foucault embarked on a variety of odd jobs in research and teaching. From 1951 to 1955, he worked as an instructor in psychology at the École Normale Supérieure at the invitation of Althusser. In Paris, he shared a flat with his brother, who was training to become a surgeon, but for three days in the week commuted to the northern town of Lille, where he took up a position at the Université Lille Nord de France, teaching psychology from 1953 to 1954. His lecturing style was looked upon positively by many of his students. Meanwhile, he continued with his work on his thesis, spending much of his time devoted to his own research in the history of psychology and psychiatry, visiting the Bibliothèque Nationale every day to read the work of psychologists like Ivan Pavlov (1849–1936), Jean Piaget (1896–1980) and Karl Jaspers (1883–1969). Undertaking research at the psychiatric institute of the Hôpital Sainte-Anne, he became an unofficial intern, studying the relationship between the doctors and the patients and aiding the experiments in the electroencephalographic laboratory. Foucault adopted many of the theories of the psychoanalyst Sigmund Freud (1856–1939), undertaking psychoanalytical interpretation of his dreams and making friends undergo Rorschach tests.

Embracing the Parisian *avant-garde*, Foucault entered into a romantic relationship with the composer Jean Barraqué (1928–1973), a prominent advocate of serialism. Together, they wished to push the boundaries of the human mind, believing that in doing so they could produce their greatest work; making heavy use of drugs, they also engaged in sado-masochistic sexual activity. In August 1953, Foucault and Barraqué went on a holiday to Italy, where the philosopher immersed himself in *Untimely Meditations* (1873–1876), a collection of four essays authored by the German philosopher Friedrich Nietzsche (1844–1900). Later describing Nietzsche's work as "a revelation", he felt that reading the book deeply affected him, and he subsequently "broke with my life" as he had formerly experienced it. Foucault would subsequently experience a groundbreaking self-revelation when watching a Parisian performance of Samuel Beckett's new play, *Waiting for Godot*, in 1953.

Taking an interest in literature, Foucault was an avid reader of the book reviews authored by the philosopher Maurice Blanchot (1907–2003), which were published in the *Nouvelle Revue Française*. Becoming enamoured with Blanchot's literary style and critical theories, in several later works he adopted Blanchot's technique of "interviewing" himself. Foucault also came across Hermann Broch's 1945 novel *The Death of*

Virgil at this time, a work that came to obsess both him and Barraqué. While the latter attempted to convert the work into an epic opera, Foucault admired Broch's text for its portrayal of death as an affirmation of life. The couple also took a mutual interest in the work of such authors as the Marquis de Sade (1740–1814), Fyodor Dostoyevsky (1821–1881), Franz Kafka (1883–1924) and Jean Genet (1910–1986), all of whose works explored the themes of sex and violence.

— Michel Foucault, 1983.

Interested in the work of Swiss psychologist Ludwig Binswanger (1881–1966), Foucault aided a young woman and family friend named Jacqueline Verdeaux in translating his works into French. Foucault was particularly interested in the work that Binswager had undertaken in studying a woman named Ellen West who, like himself, had a deep obsession with the idea of suicide, eventually killing herself. In 1954, Foucault authored an introduction to one of Binswager's papers, "Dream and Existence", in which the Frenchman put forward the idea that dreams constituted "the birth of the world" or "the heart laid bare", expressing the mind's deepest desires. That same year Foucault also published his first book, *Mental Illness and Personality* (*Maladie mentale et personnalité*), in which he exhibited his influence from both Marxist and Heideggerian thought, covering a wide range of subject matter from the reflex psychology of Pavlov to the classic psychoanalysis of Freud. Referencing the work of sociologists and anthropologists such as Émile Durkheim and Margaret Mead, he also used the book as a vehicle to present his theory that illness was culturally relative. Biographer James Miller would later note that while the book exhibited "erudition and evident intelligence", it lacked the "kind of fire and flair" which Foucault exhibited in his subsequent works. It would be largely critically ignored, receiving only one review at the time. He himself would grow to despise it, unsuccessfully attempting to prevent its republication and translation into English.

Sweden, Poland, and West Germany: 1955–1960

Foucault would spend the next five years working abroad, first in the Swedish city of Uppsala, where he took up the position of cultural diplomat at the University of Uppsala. This was a job that he had obtained through his acquaintance with the historian of religion Georges Dumézil (1898–1986), a prominent figure in French academia. At Uppsala, he was appointed a Reader in French, meaning that he was responsible for teaching both French language and literature, giving courses on such topics as "The Conception of Love in French Literature from the Marquis de Sade to Jean Genet." He was simultaneously appointed director of the Maison de France, opening the possibility of a future cultural-diplomatic career. Although finding it difficult to adjust to the "Nordic gloom" of Uppsala and its long winters, he developed close friendships with two other Frenchmen working in the city, biochemist Jean-François Miquel and physicist Jacques Papet-Lépine. In the city, he became known for his heavy alcohol consumption and reckless driving in his new Jaguar car; he also entered into romantic and sexual relationships with various men. In spring 1956, Barraqué would break from his relationship with Foucault, announcing that he wanted to leave the "vertigo of madness". In Uppsala, Foucault spent much of his spare time in the university's *Carolina Rediviva* library, where he made use of their Bibliotheca Walleriana collection of texts on the history of medicine for his ongoing research. Eventually finishing his doctoral thesis, Foucault initially hoped that it would be accepted by Uppsala University, but Sten Lindroth, a historian of science at the university, was unimpressed by his work, asserting that it was full of speculative generalisations and was a poor work of history. As such, he refused to allow Foucault to be awarded a doctorate at Uppsala. In part because of this rejection of his thesis, Foucault decided to leave Sweden and look for a post elsewhere.

In October 1958, Foucault arrived in the Polish city of Warsaw, where he was put in charge of the University of Warsaw's Centre Français. Once again, he had been recommended for the position by Dumézil. Foucault found life in Poland difficult due to the lack of material goods and services following the destruction of the Second World War. He would comment that he had moved from a "social-democratic country which functioned "well"," to a "people's democracy that functioned "badly. "" Witnessing the aftermath of the Polish October, in which students had protested against the governing Communist Party of Poland, he felt that the Polish people widely disliked their far left government, viewing them as a puppet regime of the foreign Soviet Union. Nevertheless, he felt that the university was a liberal enclave within a repressive state, although traveled to various other parts of the country giving lectures. Proving popular in Poland, he decided to adopt the position of *de facto* cultural attaché to the country. Like France and Sweden, homosexual activity was legal but socially frowned upon in Poland, and he undertook relationships with a number of men in Warsaw. One of these turned out to be a Polish government agent who hoped to trap Foucault in an embarrassing situation, which would therefore reflect badly on the French embassy. Wracked in diplomatic scandal, he was soon ordered to leave Poland for a new destination. Various positions were available in West Germany, and so Foucault decided to relocate to the city of Hamburg, where he continued to teach the same courses that he had given in Uppsala and Warsaw. Spending much of his time in the Reeperbahn red light district, he entered into a relationship with a transvestite.

***Madness and Civilization* and Kant's *Anthropology*: 1960**

— Foucault biographer David Macey, 1993.

While working in West Germany, Foucault had finally completed his doctoral thesis, *Folie et déraison: Histoire de la folie à l'âge classique* (*Madness and Insanity: History of Madness in the Classical Age*), a philosophical work based upon his studies into the history of medicine. In the book, Foucault dealt with the manner in which Western European society had dealt with madness, arguing that it was a social construct distinct from mental illness. Foucault traces the evolution of the concept of madness through three phases: the Renaissance, the "Classical Age" (the later seventeenth and most of the eighteenth centuries) and the modern experience. He argues that in the Renaissance the mad were portrayed in art as possessing a kind of wisdom, a knowledge of the limits of our world, and portrayed in literature as revealing the distinction between what men are and what they pretend to be. With the rise of the age of reason in the 17th century, madness began to be conceived of as unreason and the mad, previously consigned to society's margins, were now separated from society and confined, along with prostitutes, vagrants, blasphemers, orphans and the like, in newly created institutions all over Europe. The subsequent modern experience, Foucault argued, began at the end of the 18th century with the creation of places devoted solely to the care of the mad under the supervision of medical doctors. This was born out of a blending of two motives: the new goal of curing the mad away from the family who could not afford the necessary care at home, and the old purpose of confining undesirables for the protection of society. The work contains a number of allusions and references to the work of French poet and playwright Antonin Artaud (1896–1948), who exerted a strong influence over Foucault's thought at the time. *Histoire de la folie* was an expansive work, consisting of 943 pages of text, followed by appendixes and a bibliography. He decided to submit this work in France at the University of Paris, although the university's regulations for awarding a doctorate required the submission of both his main thesis and a shorter complementary thesis.

Obtaining a doctorate in France at the period was a multi-step process. The first step in the process was to obtain a *rapporteur*, or sponsor for the work, and Foucault found this in Georges Canguilhem. The second was to find a publisher, and as a result *Folie et déraison* would be published in French in May 1961 by the company Plon. Foucault had initially received an offer of publication from the Presses Universitaires de France, but he wanted his work to be published by a popular rather than an academic press, so that it would reach a wider audience. Hoping that his work would be picked up by Gallimard, the publishers of Jean-Paul Sartre's influential bestseller, *Being and Nothingness* (1943), he was perturbed when they rejected him, instead selecting Plon. In 1964, a heavily abridged version was published as a mass market paperback, which was then translated into English for publication the following year as *Madness and Civilization*.

Upon publication, *Folie et déraison* received a mixed reception in France and in foreign journals focusing on French affairs. It was critically acclaimed by the likes of Maurice Blochot, Michel Serres, Roland Barthes, Gaston Bachelard, and Fernand Braudel, but much to Foucault's upset, largely ignored in the leftist press. The work most notably came under attack from a young philosopher who had been a student on Foucault's psychology course at the École Normale Supérieure, Jacques Derrida (1930–2004). Derrida's critique came in the form of a lecture he gave on "The Cogito and the History of Madness" at the University of Paris on 4 March 1963, accusing Foucault of advocating metaphysics. Responding to the criticism with a vicious retort, Foucault ignored some of Derrida's points, focusing in on a criticism of how the younger philosopher had interpreted the work of René Descartes. The two would remain bitter rivals until reconciling in 1981. In the English-speaking world, the work would become a significant influence over the anti-psychiatry movement during the 1960s; Foucault himself took a mixed approach to this movement, associating with a number of figures involved in it but arguing that most of the anti-psychiatrists fundamentally misunderstood his work.

Foucault's secondary thesis involved a translation of, and commentary on, the German philosopher Immanuel Kant's 1798 work *Anthropology from a Pragmatic Point of View* (*Anthropologie in pragmatischer Hinsicht*). Much of this thesis consisted of Foucault's discussion of textual dating – an "archaeology of the Kantian text" – although he rounded off the work with an evocation of Nietzche, who had become his biggest philosophical influence. This work's *rapporteur* sponsor was his old tutor, Jean Hyppolite, who was himself well acquainted with German philosophy and who was then director of the ENS. After having both of his theses championed and reviewed, he had to undergo his public defense, the *soutenance de thèse*, on 20 May 1961. The academics responsible for reviewing his work were concerned about the unconventional nature of his major thesis; Henri Gouhier, one of the reviewers, noted that it was not a conventional work of history, making sweeping generalisations without sufficient particular argument, and that Foucault clearly "thinks in allegories". They all agreed however that the overall project was of merit, and so awarded Foucault his doctorate "despite reservations".

University of Clermont-Ferrand, *The Birth of the Clinic* and *The Order of Things*: 1960–1966

While his doctorate was being assessed, in 1960 Foucault purchased his first flat, a part of a high-rise block on the rue du Dr Finlay, off the quai de Grenelle. In October, he was offered a tenured post in philosophy at the University of Clermont-Ferrand, and over the next six years he would commute to the city every week from Paris, where he continued to live. At the time, psychology was usually subsumed within the philosophy departments in French universities, and it was this subject that Foucault was primarily responsible for teaching. Considered a "fascinating" but "rather traditional" teacher at Clermont, he was popular with his pupils. The university's philosophy department was then under the control of Jules

Vuillemin (1920–2001), who had chosen him for the position after becoming impressed by Foucault's then unpublished doctoral dissertation. After taking up his post, Foucault soon developed a friendship with Vuillemin despite their political differences; Vuillemin being a rightist and Foucault a leftist. When Vuillemin was elected to the Collège de France in 1962, he left Clermont, with Foucault taking over as the departmental head. One of the academics appointed to Clermont-Ferrand by the government was Roger Garaudy (1913–2012), a Marxist and senior figure in the French Communist Party. Foucault despised Garaudy, believing him to be stupid and disliking his dogmatic adherence to the Soviet party line. Foucault intentionally made life at the university difficult for Garaudy, highlighting his various mistakes and refusing to talk to him, leading the latter to eventually accept a transfer to Poitiers. It was in this stage of his life that Foucault met the young philosopher Daniel Defert (1937–), and they would enter into a non-monogamous relationship that would last for the rest of Foucault's life. Controversially, Foucault secured Defert a job at the university, even though other candidates for the post were better qualified.

Aside from his teaching, Foucault also maintained a keen interest in literature, having reviews published in such literary journals as *Tel Quel* and *Nouvelle Revue Française*, and sitting on the editorial board of *Critique*. In May 1963 he published a work entitled *Raymond Rousell*, which was devoted to the eponymous poet, novelist and playwright, who was one of Foucault's favourite authors. Brought out by Gallimard, it had been written in under two months, and would be described by Foucault biographer David Macey as "a very personal book" that resulted from a "love affair" with Roussel's work. It would eventually be published in English in 1983 as *Death and the Labyrinth: The World of Raymond Roussel*. It would receive few reviews, being largely ignored. That same year he also published a sequel to *Folie et déraison*, entitled *Naissance de la Clinique: une archéologie du regard médical*, subsequently translated into English as *Birth of the Clinic: An Archaeology of Medical Perception*. A shorter work than its predecessor, it focused on the changes that underwent the entire medical establishment in the late 18th and early 19th centuries. Like his preceding work, *Naissance de la Critique* was largely critically ignored, only gaining a cult following in subsequent years. Foucault was also selected to be among the "Eighteen Man Commission" that assembled between November 1963 and March 1964 to discuss university reforms that were to be implemented by Christian Fouchet, the Gaullist Minister of National Education. Upon their implementation in 1967, the reforms brought staff strikes and student protests.

In April 1966, Gallimard brought out another significant work by Foucault, *Les Mots et les choses: Une archéologie des sciences humaines* ("The words and the things"), which was later translated into English as *The Order of Things: An Archaeology of the Human Sciences*. The work explores how man came to be an object of knowledge, arguing that all periods of history have possessed certain underlying conditions of truth that constituted what was acceptable as scientific discourse. Foucault argues that these conditions of discourse have changed over time, from one period's episteme to another. Although designed for a specialist audience, the work gained press and television attention and became a surprise bestseller in France. It was during the height of interest in structuralism in 1966, and Foucault was quickly grouped with scholars such as Jacques Lacan, Claude Lévi-Strauss, and Roland Barthes as the newest, latest wave of thinkers set to topple the existentialism popularized by Jean-Paul Sartre. Although he initially accepted this description of being a "structuralist", it would not be long before Foucault changed his mind, and vehemently rejected such a description. Foucault's relationship with Sartre was strained, with the two regularly criticising one another in the press; both Sartre and his partner Simone de Beauvoir attacked Foucault and his ideas as "bourgeoisie", with Foucault retaliated against their Marxist beliefs by proclaiming that "Marxism exists in nineteenth-century thought as a fish exists in water; that is, it ceases to breathe anywhere else." Meanwhile, Foucault had been wanting to leave the university at Clermont for some time, considering both Japan and Brazil as possible destinations, and he was finally able to do so the end of the 1965–66 educational year.

University of Tunisia and *The Archaeology of Knowledge*: 1966–1970

— Michel Foucault, 1983.

Foucault then took up a position teaching psychology at the University of Tunis in the North African nation of Tunisia, which had gained independence from France in 1956. His decision to do so was in part based upon the fact that his lover, Defert, had been posted to the country as a part of his national service following the completion of his *agrégation*. Arriving in the country in September 1966, Foucault moved into the village of Sidi Bou Saïd, which was just a few kilometres away from Tunis and where Gérard Deledalle, who also worked at the university, lived with his wife. Soon after he arrived in the country, he would announce that Tunisia was "blessed by history", a nation which "deserves to live forever because it was where Hannibal and St. Augustine lived." His lectures at the university proved very popular, and were well attended. Although many of the young students were enthusiastic about his teaching, they were critical of what they believed to be his right-wing political views, viewing him as a "representative of Gaullist technocracy", even though he considered himself a leftist. Foucault was in Tunis over the course of the anti-government and pro-Palestinian riots that rocked the city in June 1967, and which would continue for the next year. Although highly critical of the violent, ultra-nationalistic and anti-semitic nature of many of the protesters, he used his status to try and prevent some of his militant leftist students from being arrested and tortured for their role in the agitation. Hiding their printing press in his own garden, he tried to testify on their behalf at their trials, but was prevented when the trials became closed-door events.

While in Tunis, Foucault had continued to write. Inspired by a correspondence with the surrealist artist René Magritte, Foucault set about writing a book upon the impressionist artist Eduard Manet, but it was never completed.

He was still in Tunis during the May 1968 student riots, where he was profoundly affected by a local student revolt earlier in the same year. In the Autumn of 1968 he returned to France, where he published *L'archéologie du savoir* (*The Archaeology of Knowledge*) – a methodological treatise that included a response to his critics – in 1969.

In the aftermath of 1968, the French government created a new experimental university, Paris VIII, at Vincennes and appointed Foucault the first head of its philosophy department in December of that year. Foucault appointed mostly young leftist academics (such as Judith Miller) whose radicalism provoked the Ministry of Education, who objected to the fact that many of the course titles contained the phrase "Marxist-Leninist," and who decreed that students from Vincennes would not be eligible to become secondary school teachers. Foucault notoriously also joined students in occupying administration buildings and fighting with police.

Collège de France: 1970–

Foucault's tenure at Vincennes was short-lived, as in 1970 he was elected to France's most prestigious academic body, the Collège de France, as Professor of the History of Systems of Thought. His political involvement increased, and his partner Defert joined the ultra-Maoist Gauche Proletarienne (GP). Foucault helped found the Prison Information Group (French: *Groupe d'Information sur les Prisons* or GIP) to provide a way for prisoners to voice their concerns. This coincided with Foucault's turn to the study of disciplinary institutions, with a book, *Surveiller et Punir* (*Discipline and Punish*), which "narrates" the micro-power structures that developed in Western societies since the 18th century, with a special focus on prisons and schools.

Later life

In the late 1970s, political activism in France trailed off with the disillusionment of many left wing intellectuals. A number of young Maoists abandoned their beliefs to become the so-called New Philosophers, often citing Foucault as their major influence, a status Foucault had mixed feelings about. Foucault in this period embarked on a six-volume project *The History of Sexuality*, which he never completed. Its first volume was published in French as *La Volonté de Savoir* (1976), then in English as *The History of Sexuality: An Introduction* (1978). The second and third volumes did not appear for another eight years, and they surprised readers by their subject matter (classical Greek and Latin texts), approach and style, particularly Foucault's focus on the human subject, a concept that some mistakenly believed he had previously neglected.

Foucault began to spend more time in the United States, at the University at Buffalo (where he had lectured on his first ever visit to the United States in 1970) and especially at UC Berkeley. In 1975 he took LSD at Zabriskie Point in Death Valley National Park, later calling it the best experience of his life.

Iranian Revolution

In 1979 Foucault made two tours of Iran, undertaking extensive interviews with political protagonists in support of the new interim government established soon after the Iranian Revolution. In the tradition of Nietzsche and Georges Bataille, Foucault had embraced the artist who pushed the limits of rationality, and he wrote with great passion in defense of irrationalities that broke boundaries. In 1978, Foucault found such transgressive powers in the revolutionary figures Ayatollah Khomeini, Ali Shariati and the millions who risked death as they followed them in the course of the revolution. Both Foucault and the revolutionaries were highly critical of modernity and sought a new form of politics, they both also looked up to those who risked their lives for ideals; and both looked to the past for inspiration. Later on when Foucault went to Iran "to be there at the birth of a new form of ideas," he wrote that the new "Muslim" style of politics could signal the beginning of a new form of "political spirituality," not just for the Middle East, but also for Europe, which had adopted the practice of secular politics ever since the French Revolution. Foucault recognized the enormous power of the new discourse of militant Islam, not just for Iran, but for the world. He wrote:

As an Islamic movement, it can set the entire region afire, overturn the most unstable regimes, and disturb the most solid. Islam which is not simply a religion, but an entire way of life, an adherence to a history and a civilization, has a good chance to become a gigantic powder keg, at the level of hundreds of millions of men. . . Indeed, it is also important to recognize that the demand for the 'legitimate rights of the Palestinian people' hardly stirred the Arab peoples. What it be if this cause encompassed the dynamism of an Islamic movement, something much stronger than those with a Marxist, Leninist, or Maoist character? ("A Powder Keg Called Islam")

During his two trips to Iran, Foucault was commissioned as a special correspondent of a leading Italian newspaper and his articles appeared on the front page of that paper. His many essays on Iran, published in the Italian newspaper *Corriere della Sera*, only appeared in French in 1994 and then in English in 2005. These essays caused some controversy, with some commentators arguing that Foucault was insufficiently critical of the new regime. The more common attempts to bracket out Foucault's writings on Iran as "miscalculations," reminds some authors of what Foucault himself had criticized in his well known 1969 essay, "What is an Author?" Foucault believed that when we include certain works in an author's career and exclude others that were written in a "different style," or were "inferior" (Foucault 1969, 111), we create a stylistic unity and a theoretical coherence. This is done by privileging certain writings as authentic and excluding others that do not fit our view of what the author ought to be: "The author is therefore the ideological figure by which one marks the manner in which we fear the proliferation of meaning" (Foucault 1969, 110). This controversy is frequently discussed in the Foucault literature.

Illness and death: 1983–1984

In the philosopher's later years, interpreters of Foucault's work attempted to engage with the problems presented by the fact that the late Foucault seemed in tension with the philosopher's earlier work. When this issue was raised in a 1982 interview, Foucault remarked "When people say, 'Well, you thought this a few years ago and now you say something else,' my answer is… [laughs] 'Well, do you think I have worked hard all those years to say the same thing and not to be changed?'" He refused to identify himself as a philosopher, historian, structuralist, or Marxist, maintaining that "The main interest in life and work is to become someone else that you were not in the beginning." In a similar vein, he preferred not to state that he was presenting a coherent and timeless block of knowledge; he rather desired his books "to be a kind of toolbox others can rummage through to find a tool they can use however they wish in their own area… I don't write for an audience, I write for users, not readers."

During these trips to California, Foucault spent many evenings in the gay scene of the San Francisco Bay Area. He frequented a number of sado-masochistic bathhouses, engaging in sexual intercourse with other patrons. He would praise sado-masochistic activity in interviews with the gay press, describing it as "the real creation of new possibilities of pleasure, which people had no idea about previously." The American academic James Miller would later claim that Foucault's experiences in the gay sadomasochism community during the time he taught at Berkeley directly influenced his political and philosophical works. Miller's ideas have been rebuked by certain Foucault scholars as being either simply misdirected, a sordid reading of his life and works, or as a politically motivated, intentional misreading.

At one point, Foucault contracted the HIV virus, which would eventually develop into AIDS. Little was known of the disease at the time; the first cases had only been identified in 1980, and it had only been named in 1982. In the summer of 1983, he noticed that he had a persistent dry cough; friends in Paris became concerned that he may have contracted the HIV/AIDS virus then sweeping the San Francisco gay population, but Foucault insisted that he had nothing more than a pulmonary infection that would clear up when he spent the autumn of 1983 in California. It was only when hospitalised that Foucault was diagnosed with AIDS; placed on antibiotics, he was able to deliver a final set of lectures at the Collège de France. Foucault entered Paris' Hôpital de la Salpêtrière – the same institution that he had studied in *Madness and Civilisation* – on 9 June 1984, with neurological symptoms complicated by septicemia. He died in the hospital at 1:15pm on 25 June.

On 26 June, the newspaper *Libération* – associated with Foucault for much of his life – announced his death, also highlighting the rumour that it had been brought on by AIDS. The following day, *Le Monde* publicly issued a medical bulletin that had been cleared by his family; it made no reference to the HIV/AIDS virus. On 29 June, Foucault's *la levée du corps* ceremony was held, in which the coffin was carried from the morgue. Taking place in the rear courtyard of the Hôpital de la Salpêtrière, it was attended by hundreds of admirers who had seen the event advertised in *Le Monde*, including left wing activists like Yves Montand and Simone Signoret and academics such as Jacques Derrida, Paul Veyne, Pierre Bourdieu and Georges Dumézil. Foucault's friend Gilles Deleuze gave a speech, with the words coming from the preface to the final two volumes of *The History of Sexuality*. Soon after his death, Foucault's partner Daniel Defert founded the first national AIDS organisation in France, which he called AIDES; a pun on the French language word for "help" (*aide*) and the English language acronym for the disease. On the second anniversary of Foucault's death, Defert agreed to publicly announce that Foucault's death was AIDS-related, doing so in the California-based gay magazine, *The Advocate*.

Personal life

Foucault's first biographer, Didier Eribon, described the philosopher as "a complex, many-sided character", and that "under one mask there is always another". He also noted that he exhibited an "enormous capacity for work". At the ENS, Foucault's classmates unanimously summed him up as a figure who was both "disconcerting and strange" and "a passionate worker". His personality would change as he aged however; Eribon noted that while he was a "tortured adolescent", post-1960, he had become "a radiant man, relaxed and cheerful", even being described by those who worked with him as a dandy.

Foucault was a fan of classical music, particularly enjoying the work of Johann Sebastian Bach and Wolfgang Amadeus Mozart.

Politically, Foucault remained a leftist throughout his life, but his particular stance within the left often changed. In the early 1950s he had been a member of the French Communist Party, although never adopted an orthodox Marxist viewpoint and left the party after three years, disgusted by the prejudice towards Jews and homosexuals within its ranks. After spending some time working in Poland, then governed as a socialist state by the Communist Party of Poland, he became further disillusioned with communism, and by the early 1960s was considered to be "violently anticommunist".

Thought

Philip Stokes, *Philosophy: 100 Essential Thinkers*, 2004.

Philosopher Philip Stokes of the University of Reading noted that overall, Foucault's work was "dark and pessimistic", but that it did leave some room for optimism, in that it illustrates how the discipline of philosophy can be used to highlight areas of domination. In doing so, Stokes claimed, we are able to understand how we are being dominated and strive to build social structures that minimize this risk of domination.

Major Works

Madness and Civilization

The English edition of *Madness and Civilization* is an abridged version of *Folie et déraison: Histoire de la folie à l'âge classique*, originally published in 1961. A full English translation titled *The History of Madness* has since been published by Routledge in 2006. "Folie et deraison" originated as Foucault's doctoral dissertation; this was Foucault's first major book, mostly written while he was the Director of the Maison de France in Sweden. It examines ideas, practices, institutions, art, and literature relating to madness in Western history.

Foucault begins his history in the Middle Ages, noting the social and physical exclusion of lepers. He argues that with the gradual disappearance of leprosy, madness came to occupy this excluded position. The ship of fools in the 15th century is a literary version of one such exclusionary practice, namely that of sending mad people away in ships. In 17th century Europe, in a movement Foucault famously calls the "Great Confinement," "unreasonable" members of the population were institutionalised. In the 18th century, madness came to be seen as the reverse of Reason, and, finally, in the 19th century as mental illness.

Foucault also argues that madness was silenced by Reason, losing its power to signify the limits of social order and to point to the truth. He examines the rise of scientific and "humanitarian" treatments of the insane, notably at the hands of Philippe Pinel and Samuel Tuke who he suggests started the conceptualization of madness as 'mental illness'. He claims that these new treatments were in fact no less controlling than previous methods. Pinel's treatment of the mad amounted to an extended aversion therapy, including such treatments as freezing showers and use of a straitjacket. In Foucault's view, this treatment amounted to repeated brutality until the pattern of judgment and punishment was internalized by the victim.

The Birth of the Clinic

Foucault's second major book, *The Birth of the Clinic: An Archaeology of Medical Perception* (*Naissance de la clinique: une archéologie du regard médical*) was published in 1963 in France, and translated to English in 1973. Picking up from *Madness and Civilization*, *The Birth of the Clinic* traces the development of the medical profession, and specifically the institution of the *clinique* (translated as "clinic", but here largely referring to teaching hospitals). Its motif is the concept of the medical *regard* (translated by Alan Sheridan as "medical gaze"), traditionally limited to small, specialized institutions such as hospitals and prisons, but which Foucault examines as subjecting wider social spaces, governing the population *en masse*.

Death and The Labyrinth

Death and the Labyrinth: The World of Raymond Roussel was published in 1963, and translated into English in 1986. It is Foucault's only book-length work on literature. Foucault described it as "by far the book I wrote most easily, with the greatest pleasure, and most rapidly." Foucault explores theory, criticism, and psychology with reference to the texts of Raymond Roussel, one of the fathers of experimental writing.

The Order of Things

Foucault's *Les Mots et les choses. Une archéologie des sciences humaines* was published in 1966. It was translated into English in 1970 under the title *The Order of Things: An Archaeology of the Human Sciences*. Foucault had preferred *L'Ordre des choses* for the original French title, but changed it as there was already another book by that name. The work broadly aims to provide an anti-humanist *excavation* of the human sciences, such as sociology and psychology. It opens with an extended discussion of Diego Velázquez's painting *Las Meninas* and the painting's complex arrangement of sight-lines, hiddenness, and appearance. It then develops its central thesis: all periods of history have possessed specific underlying conditions of truth that constituted what could be expressed as discourse (for example art, science, culture, etc.). Foucault argues that these conditions of discourse have changed over time, in major and relatively sudden shifts, from one period's *episteme* to another. Foucault's Nietzschean critique of Enlightenment values in *Les mots et les choses* has been very influential in cultural studies and social work scholarship. It is in this book that Foucault claims that "man is only a recent invention" and that the "end of man" is at hand.

The book made Foucault a prominent intellectual figure in France.

The Archaeology of Knowledge

Published in 1969, this volume was Foucault's main excursion into methodology, written as an outcome of discussions with the French Circle of Epistemology. The book explains the methodology of his previous theoretical works. Taking its point of departure in the French epistemological tradition, it makes few references to Anglo-American analytical philosophy except as to speech act theory, from which Foucault distances himself.

Foucault directs his analysis toward the "statement" (*énoncé*), which is the rules that render an expression (that is, a phrase, a proposition, or a speech act) discursively meaningful. This concept of meaning differs from the concept of signification: Though an expression is signifying, for instance "The gold mountain is in California", it may nevertheless be *discursively meaningless* and therefore have no existence within a certain discourse. For this reason, the "statement" is an *existence function* for *discursive meaning*. Being rules, the "statement" has a very special meaning in the *Archaeology*: it is *not* the expression itself, but the rules which make an expression discursively meaningful. These rules are not the syntax and semantics that makes an expression signifying. It is additional rules. In contrast to structuralists, Foucault demonstrates that the semantic and syntactic structures do not suffice to determine the discursive meaning of an expression. Depending on whether or not it complies with these rules of discursive meaning, a grammatically correct phrase may lack discursive meaning or, inversely, a grammatically incorrect sentence may be discursively meaningful - even meaningless letters, e.g. "QWERT" may have discursive meaning. Thus, the meaning of expressions depends on the conditions in which they emerge and exist within a field of discourse; the discursive meaning of an expression is reliant on the succession of statements that precede and follow it. In short, the "statements" Foucault analysed are not propositions, phrases, or speech acts. Rather, "statements" constitute a network of rules establishing which expressions are discursively meaningful, and these rules are the preconditions for signifying propositions, utterances, or speech acts to have discursive meaning. However, "statements" are also 'events', because, like other rules, they appear (or disappear) at some time.

Foucault aims his analysis towards a huge organized dispersion of statements, called *discursive formations*. Foucault reiterates that the analysis he is outlining is only one possible procedure, and that he is not seeking to displace other ways of analysing discourse or render them as invalid.

According to Dreyfus and Rabinow, Foucault not only brackets out issues of truth (cf. Husserl), he also brackets out issues of meaning. However, Foucault does not bracket out discursive meaning. But, focusing on discursive meaning, Foucault did not look for a deeper meaning underneath discourse or for the source of meaning in some transcendental subject. Instead, Foucault analyzes the discursive and practical conditions for the existence of truth and discursive meaning. To show the principles of production of truth and discursive meaning in various discursive formations, he details how truth claims emerge during various epochs on the basis of what was actually said and written during these periods. He particularly describes the Renaissance, the Age of Enlightenment, and the 20th century. He strives to avoid all interpretation and to depart from the goals of hermeneutics. This does not mean that Foucault denounces truth and discursive meaning, but just that truth and discursive meaning depend on the historical discursive and practical means of truth and meaning production. For instance, although they were radically different during Enlightenment as opposed to Modernity, there were indeed discursive meaning, truth, and correct treatment of madness during both epochs (*Madness and Civilization*). This posture allows Foucault to denounce *a priori* concepts of the nature of the human subject and focus on the role of discursive practices in constituting subjectivity.

Foucault's relation to structuralism is ambiguous. However, in the preface to the English translation of Les Mots et les Choses (1970), he clearly disavowed structuralism:

In France certain half-witted 'commentators' persist in labelling me a 'structuralist'. I have been unable to get it into their tiny minds that I have used none of the methods, concepts, or key terms that characterize structural analysis.

Whereas structuralists search for homogeneity in a discursive entity, Foucault focuses on differences. Instead of asking what constitutes the specificity of European thought he asks what constitutes the differences developed within it and over time. Therefore, as a historical method, he refuses to examine statements outside of their historical context: the discursive formation. The meaning of a statement depends on the general rules that characterize the discursive formation to which it belongs. A discursive formation continually generates new statements, and some of these usher in changes in the discursive formation that may or may not be adopted. Therefore, to describe a discursive formation, Foucault also focuses on expelled and forgotten discourses that never happened to change the discursive formation (the genealogical analysis). Their differences from the dominant discourse also describe it. In this way one can describe specific systems that determine which types of statements emerge.

In his work *Foucault* (1986), Deleuze describes *The Archaeology of Knowledge* as "the most decisive step yet taken in the theory-practice of multiplicities." The book was not as successful as *The Order of Things*.

Discipline and Punish

Discipline and Punish: The Birth of the Prison was translated into English in 1977, from the French *Surveiller et punir: Naissance de la prison*, published in 1975. It details the emergence of prisons as in Europe and explores Foucault's views on power. The book is among Foucault's most successful and influential works.

The book opens with a graphic description of the brutal public execution in 1757 of Robert-François Damiens, who attempted to kill Louis XV. Against this it juxtaposes a colourless prison timetable from just over 80 years later. Foucault then inquires how such a change in French society's punishment of convicts could have developed in such a short time. These are snapshots of two contrasting types of Foucault's "Technologies of Punishment." The first type, "Monarchical Punishment," involves the repression of the populace through brutal public displays of executions and torture. The second, "Disciplinary Punishment," is what Foucault says is practiced in the modern era. Disciplinary punishment gives "professionals" (psychologists, programme facilitators, parole officers, etc.) power over the prisoner, most notably in that the prisoner's length of stay depends on the professionals' judgment. Foucault goes on to argue that Disciplinary punishment leads to self-policing by the populace as opposed to brutal displays of authority from the Monarchical period.

Foucault argues between the 17th and 18th centuries a new, more subtle form of power was being exercised transnationally. He calls this form of power discipline. Soldiers could be made and formed rather than just being chosen because of their natural characteristics. Knowledge and power are central to Foucault's analysis. He questions common concepts like justice or equality and asks where these concepts originated and who they benefit. The process of observing and evaluating individuals leads to more and more knowledge about peoples.

Foucault also compares modern society with Jeremy Bentham's "Panopticon" design for prisons (which was unrealized in its original form, but nonetheless influential): in the Panopticon, a single guard can watch over many prisoners while the guard remains unseen. Ancient prisons have been replaced by clear and visible ones, but Foucault cautions that "visibility is a trap." It is through this visibility, Foucault writes, that modern society exercises its controlling systems of power and knowledge (terms Foucault believed to be so fundamentally connected that he often combined them in a single hyphenated concept, "power-knowledge"). Increasing visibility leads to power located on an increasingly individualized level, shown by the possibility for institutions to track individuals throughout their lives. Foucault suggests that a "carceral continuum" runs through modern society, from the maximum security prison, through secure accommodation, probation, social workers, police, and teachers, to our everyday working and domestic lives. All are connected by the (witting or unwitting) supervision (surveillance, application of norms of acceptable behaviour) of some humans by others.

The History of Sexuality

Three volumes of *The History of Sexuality* were published before Foucault's death in 1984. The first and most referenced volume, *The Will to Knowledge* (previously known as *An Introduction* in English – *Histoire de la sexualité, 1: la volonté de savoir* in French) was published in France in 1976, and translated in 1977, focusing primarily on the last two centuries, and the functioning of sexuality as an analytics of power related to the emergence of a science of sexuality (*scientia sexualis*) and the emergence of biopower in the West. In this volume he attacks the "repressive hypothesis", the widespread belief that we have "repressed" our natural sexual drives, particularly since the 19th century. He proposes that what is thought of as "repression" of sexuality actually constituted sexuality as a core feature of human identities, and produced a proliferation of discourse on the subject.

The second two volumes, *The Use of Pleasure* (*Histoire de la sexualité, II: l'usage des plaisirs*) and *The Care of the Self* (*Histoire de la sexualité, III: le souci de soi*) dealt with the role of sex in Greek and Roman antiquity. Both were published in 1984, the year of Foucault's death, with the second volume being translated in 1985, and the third in 1986. In his lecture series from 1979 to 1980 Foucault extended his analysis of government to its 'wider sense of techniques and procedures designed to direct the behaviour of men', which involved a new consideration of the 'examination of conscience' and confession in early Christian literature. These themes of early Christian literature seemed to dominate Foucault's work, alongside his study of Greek and Roman literature, until the end of his life. However, Foucault's death left the work incomplete, and the planned fourth volume of his *History of Sexuality* on Christianity was never published. The fourth volume was to be entitled *Confessions of the Flesh* (*Les aveux de la chair*). The volume was almost complete before Foucault's death and a copy of it is privately held in the Foucault archive. It cannot be published under the restrictions of Foucault's estate.

Lectures

In 1970 Foucault began a schedule of weekly public lectures and seminars during the first three months of each year at the Collège de France as the condition of his tenure as professor there. These continued each year except 1977 until his death in 1984. The lectures were tape-recorded and Foucault's notes also survive. In 1997 the lectures began to be published in French. Of the first nine volumes to be published, eight have been translated into English: *Psychiatric Power 1973–1974*, *Abnormal 1974–1975*, *Society Must Be Defended 1975–1976*, *Security, Territory, Population 1977–1978*, *The Birth of Biopolitics 1978-1979*, *The Hermeneutics of the Subject 1981–1982*, *The Government of Self and Others 1982–1983*, and *The Courage of Truth 1983-1984*.

Society Must Be Defended and *Security, Territory, Population* pursued an analysis of the broader relationship between security and biopolitics, explicitly politicizing the question of the birth of humankind raised in *The Order of Things*. In *Security, Territory, Population*, Foucault outlines his theory of governmentality, and demonstrates the distinction between sovereignty, discipline, and governmentality as distinct modalities of state power. He argues that governmental state power can be genealogically linked to the 17th century state philosophy of *raison d'etat* and, ultimately, to the medieval Christian 'pastoral' concept of power. Notes of some of Foucault's lectures from University of California, Berkeley in 1983 have also appeared as *Fearless Speech*.

Influence

Foucault's discussions on power and discourse have inspired many critical theorists, who believe that Foucault's analysis of power structures could aid the struggle against inequality. They claim that through discourse analysis, hierarchies may be uncovered and questioned by way of analyzing the corresponding fields of knowledge through which they are legitimated. This is one of the ways that Foucault's work is linked to critical theory.

Foucault was listed as the most cited scholar in the humanities in 2007 by the *ISI Web of Science*.

Criticisms

Philosopher Jürgen Habermas has described Foucault as a "crypto-normativist", covertly reliant on the very Enlightenment principles he attempts to deconstruct. Central to this problem, Habermas argues, is the way Foucault seemingly attempts to remain *both* Kantian and Nietzschean in his approach.

Philosopher Richard Rorty has argued that Foucault's 'archaeology of knowledge' is fundamentally negative, and thus fails to adequately establish any 'new' theory of knowledge *per se*. Rather, Foucault simply provides a few valuable maxims regarding the reading of history. Says Rorty:

Philosopher Roger Scruton argued that Foucault was a "fraud" because he exploited known difficulties of philosophy in order to "disguise unexamined premises as hard-won conclusions".

Source http://en.wikipedia.org/wiki/Michel_Foucault

Patrick Kelly (fashion designer)

Patrick Kelly (c. September 24, 1954 – January 1, 1990) was a Vicksburg, Mississippi, U.S. born. Kelly studied art at Jackson State University and than attended Parsons Design NYC. While living in Atlanta Kelly sold recycled clothes and working with out pay at Yves Saint Laurent chairman Pierre Bergé, who later in 1988, sponsored Kelly. Paris-based women's wear designer and a founder of the fashion house Patrick Kelly Paris. Kelly achieved his greatest commercial success in the late 1980s and in 1988 Kelly became both the first American and the first person of color to be admitted as a member of the Chambre syndicale du prêt-à-porter des couturiers et des créateurs de mode. Kelly died at age 35 on New Year's Day, 1990. Originally Kelly's causes of death were reported to be bone marrow disease and a brain tumor, but the actual cause of death is now acknowledged to be complications of AIDS.

Working from Paris, Kelly produced collections for five years, beginning in 1985 and continuing until his death in 1990. After receiving financial backing from the U.S. based fashion conglomerate Warnaco in July, 1987, Kelly was able to hire a staff and eventually achieve wholesale sales of US $7.2 million per year. Kelly's designs were sold in upscale retailers including Henri Bendel, Bergdorf Goodman and Bloomingdale's and were worn by celebrities including Isabella Rossellini, Bette Davis, Cicely Tyson and Grace Jones. Kelly's designs frequently incorporated bright colors, were often embellished with ribbons and buttons and suggested a sense of whimsy and joy while sometimes addressing difficult issues of race. This was pointed out by the giving his audience a tiny brown doll with molded black hair that could be most accurately described as a pickaninny. Kelly also used culture using motifs such as watermelon and the golliwog. He was known to walk the runway in baggy overalls and used a large spray paint heart as the background to his fashion shows. }</ref>

In 2004, The Brooklyn Museum presented *Patrick Kelly: A Retrospective*, a show featuring more than sixty Kelly designs.

Source http://en.wikipedia.org/wiki/Patrick_Kelly_(fashion_designer)

Rémi Laurent

Rémi Laurent

Born	Rémi François Simon Laurent October 12, 1957 Suresnes, Paris, France
Died	November 14, 1989 (aged 32) Paris, France
Cause of death	HIV related illness
Occupation	Actor
Years active	1976-1987

Rémi Laurent (12 October 1957, Suresnes - 14 November 1989, Paris) was a French actor, best known for playing the son Laurent in *La Cage aux Folles*. He died from an HIV related illness in 1989.

Filmography

La Princesse surgelée (1987)
Black Mic Mac (1986) - L'inspecteur adjoint
Le Cadeau (Bankers Also Have Souls aka. *The Gift)* (1982) - Laurent
Une glace avec deux boules ou je le dis à maman (1982) - Bernard
Les Plouffe (The Plouffe Family) (1981) - Denis Boucher
La Cassure (1981)
Tous vedettes (All Stars) (1980) - Laurent
C'est dingue... mais on y va (1979) - Nicolas
La Cage aux folles (1978) - Laurent Baldi
Les Seize ans de Jérémy Millet (1978)
Arrête ton char... bidasse! (1977) - Francis
Dis bonjour à la dame (1977) - David Ferry
À nous les petites Anglaises (Let's Get Those English Girls) (1976) - Alain

Biography

Source http://en.wikipedia.org/wiki/Rémi_Laurent

Rudolf Nureyev

Rudolf Nureyev

Rudolf Nureyev in 1973 by Allan Warren

Born	Rudolf Khametovich Nureyev 17 March 1938 near Irkutsk, Russian SFSR, Soviet Union
Died	6 January 1993 (aged 54) Levallois-Perret, France
Cause of death	AIDS
Nationality	Russian
Ethnicity	Bashkir-Tatar
Citizenship	U.K.
Alma mater	Kirov Ballet School
Occupation	ballet dancer, choreographer
Years active	1958–1992
Partner(s)	Erik Bruhn (1961–1986)
Website	www.nureyev.org

Rudolf Khametovich Nureyev (Bashkir: Рудольф Хәмит улы Нуриев, Tatar: Rudolf Xämit ulı Nuriev, Russian: Рудо́льф Хаме́тович Нуре́ев) (17 March 1938 – 6 January 1993) was a dancer of ballet and modern dance, one of the most celebrated of the 20th century. Nureyev's artistic skills explored expressive areas of the dance, providing a new role to the male ballet dancer who once served only as support to the women.

Originally a Soviet citizen, Nureyev defected to the West in 1961, despite KGB efforts to stop him. According to KGB archives studied by Peter Watson, Nikita Khrushchev personally signed an order to have Nureyev killed.

Early life and career at the Kirov Ballet

Nureyev was born on a Trans-Siberian train near Irkutsk, Siberia, Soviet Union, while his mother Feride was travelling to Vladivostok, where his father Hamit, a Red Army political commissar, was stationed. He was raised as the only son in a Bashkir-Tatar family in a village near Ufa in Soviet republic of Bashkortostan. When his mother took him and his sisters into a performance of the ballet "Song of the Cranes", he fell in love with dance. As a child he was encouraged to dance in Bashkir folk performances and his precocity was soon noticed by teachers who encouraged him to train in Leningrad. On a tour stop in Moscow with a local ballet company, Nureyev auditioned for the Bolshoi ballet company and was accepted. However, he felt that the Kirov Ballet school was the best, so he left the local touring company and bought a ticket to Leningrad.

Owing to the disruption of Soviet cultural life caused by World War II, Nureyev was unable to enroll in a major ballet school until 1955, aged 17, when he was accepted by the Leningrad Choreographic School, the associate school of the Kirov Ballet.

Alexander Ivanovich Pushkin took an interest in him professionally and allowed Nureyev to live with him and his wife. Upon graduation, Nureyev continued with the Kirov and went on to become a soloist.

In his three years with the Kirov, he danced fifteen rôles, usually opposite his partner, Ninel Kurgapkina, with whom he was very well paired, although she was almost a decade older than he was. He became one of the Soviet Union's best-known dancers and was allowed to travel outside the Soviet Union, when he danced in Vienna at the International Youth Festival. Not long after, he was told by the Ministry of Culture that he would not be allowed to go abroad again.

Defection

Rudolf Nureyev at his defection from Soviet Union 1961.

By the late 1950s, Nureyev had become a sensation in the Soviet Union. Yet, as the Kirov Ballet was preparing to go on a European tour, Nureyev's rebellious character and a non-conformist attitude quickly made him the unlikely candidate for a trip to the West, which was to be of crucial importance to the Soviet government's ambitions to portray their cultural supremacy. However, in 1961, the Kirov's leading male dancer, Konstantin Sergeyev, was injured, and Nureyev was chosen to replace him on the Kirov's European tour. In Paris, his performances electrified audiences and critics. Oliver Merlin in *Le Monde* wrote,

I will never forget his arrival running across the back of the stage, and his catlike way of holding himself opposite the ramp. He wore a white sash over an ultramarine costume, had large wild eyes and hollow cheeks under a turban topped with a spray of feathers, bulging thighs, immaculate tights. This was already Nijinsky in *Firebird*.

Nureyev was seen to have broken the rules about mingling with foreigners, which alarmed the Kirov's management. The KGB wanted to send him back to the Soviet Union immediately. As a subterfuge, they told him that he would not travel with the company to London to continue the tour because he was needed to dance at a special performance in the Kremlin. When that didn't work they told him his mother had fallen severely ill and he needed to come home immediately to see her. He knew these were lies and believed that if he returned to the USSR, he would likely be imprisoned, because KGB agents had been investigating him.

On 16 June 1961 at the Le Bourget Airport in Paris, Rudolf Nureyev defected with the help of French police and a Parisian socialite friend – Clara Saint. Within a week, he was signed up by the Grand Ballet du Marquis de Cuevas and was performing *The Sleeping Beauty* with Nina Vyroubova. On a tour of Denmark he met Erik Bruhn, soloist at the Royal Danish Ballet who became his lover, his closest friend and his protector until Bruhn's death in 1986.

Although he petitioned the Soviet government for many years to be allowed to visit his mother, he was not allowed to do so until 1987, when his mother was dying and Mikhail Gorbachev consented to the visit. In 1989, he was invited to dance the role of *James* in *La Sylphide* with the Kirov Ballet at the Maryinsky theatre in Leningrad. The visit gave him the opportunity to see many of the teachers and colleagues he had not seen since he defected.

Royal Ballet

Nureyev's first appearance in Britain was at a ballet matinée organised by The Royal Ballet's Prima Ballerina Dame Margot Fonteyn. The event was held in aid of the Royal Academy of Dance, a classical ballet teaching organisation of which she was President. He danced *Poeme Tragique*, a solo choreographed by Frederick Ashton, and the *Black Swan pas de deux* from *Swan Lake*.

Dame Ninette de Valois offered him a contract to join The Royal Ballet as Principal Dancer. His first appearance with the company was partnering Margot Fonteyn in *Giselle* on 21 February 1962. Fonteyn and Nureyev would go on to form a partnership. Nureyev stayed with the Royal Ballet until 1970, when he was promoted to Principal Guest Artist, enabling him to concentrate on his increasing schedule of international guest appearances and tours. He continued to perform regularly with The Royal Ballet until committing his future to the Paris Opera Ballet in the 1980s.

Nureyev and his dance partnerships

Rudolf Nureyev and Margot Fonteyn in the *Grand adage* from Nureyev's staging of the Petipa/Minkus *The Kingdom of the Shades* for the Royal Ballet, London, 1963.

Rudolph Nureyev and Margot Fonteyn became longstanding dance partners and continued to dance together for many years after Nureyev's departure from the Royal Ballet. Their last performance together was in *Baroque Pas de Trois* on 16 September 1988 when Fonteyn was 69, Nureyev was aged 50, with Carla Fracci also starring, aged 52. Nureyev once said of Fonteyn that they danced with "one body, one soul".

Together Nureyev and Fonteyn premiered Sir Frederick Ashton's ballet *Marguerite and Armand*, a ballet danced to Liszt's Piano Sonata in B minor, which became their signature piece. Kenneth MacMillan was forced to allow them to premiere his *Romeo and Juliet*, which was intended for two other dancers, Lynn Seymour and Christopher Gable. Films exist of their partnership in *Les Sylphides*, *Swan Lake*, *Romeo and Juliet*, and other roles.

Nureyev danced with many of the top ballerinas of his time. He celebrated another long-time partnership with Prima Ballerina Assoluta Eva Evdokimova. They first appeared together in *La Sylphide* (1971) and in 1975 he selected her as his *Sleeping Beauty* in his staging for London Festival Ballet. Evdokimova remained his partner of choice for many guest appearances and tours across the globe with "Nureyev and Friends" for more than fifteen years.

Film and television

In 1962, Nureyev made his screen debut in a film version of *Les Sylphides*. In 1977 he played Rudolph Valentino in Ken Russell's *Valentino*, but he decided against an acting career in order to branch into modern dance with the Dutch National Ballet in 1968. In 1972, Sir Robert Helpmann invited him to tour Australia with his own production of *Don Quixote*, his directorial debut. The film version (1973) features Nureyev, Lucette Aldous as *Kitri*, Helpmann as *Don Quixote* and artists of the Australian Ballet.

During the 1970s, Nureyev appeared in several films and toured through the United States in a revival of the Broadway musical *The King and I*. He was one of the guest stars on the television series *The Muppet Show* where he danced in a parody called *Swine Lake*, sang *Baby, It's Cold Outside* in a sauna duet with *Miss Piggy*, and sang and tap-danced in the show's finale, *Top Hat, White Tie and Tails*. It is an appearance that is credited with making Jim Henson's series become one of the sought after programs to appear in. In 1981, Thames Television filmed a documentary with Nureyev, including a candid interview, as well as access to him in the studio, rehearsing. In 1982, he became a naturalized Austrian. In 1983 he had a non-dancing role in the movie *Exposed* with Nastassja Kinski.

Director of the Paris Opera

Ballet

In 1983, he was appointed director of the Paris Opera Ballet, where, as well as directing, he continued to dance and to promote younger dancers. He remained there as a dancer and chief of choreography until 1989. Among the dancers he groomed were Sylvie Guillem, Isabelle Guérin, Manuel Legris, Elisabeth Maurin, Élisabeth Platel, Charles Jude, and Monique Loudieres. Despite advancing illness towards the end of his tenure, he worked tirelessly, staging new versions of old standbys and commissioning some of the most ground-breaking choreographic works of his time. His own *Romeo and Juliet* was a popular success.

Personality

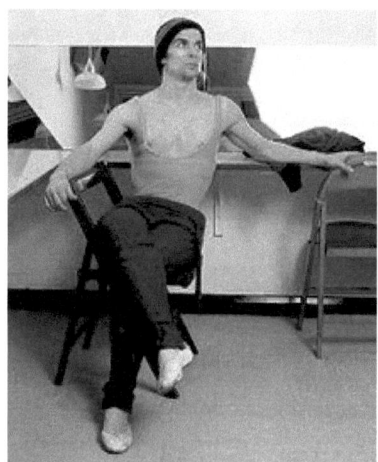

Nureyev in dressing room in 1974, by Allan Warren.

Nureyev did not have much patience with rules, limitations and hierarchical order and had at times a volatile temper. His impatience mainly showed itself when the failings of others interfered with his work. Most ballerinas with whom he danced, including Antoinette Sibley, Gelsey Kirkland and Annette Page paid tribute to him as a considerate partner.

He socialized with Gore Vidal, Freddie Mercury, Jackie Kennedy Onassis, Mick Jagger, Liza Minnelli, Andy Warhol and Talitha Pol, but developed an intolerance for celebrities. He kept up old friendships in and out of the ballet world for decades, and was considered to be a loyal and generous friend. He was known as extremely generous to many ballerinas, who credit him with helping them during difficult times. In particular, the Canadian ballerina Lynn Seymour – distressed when she was denied the opportunity to premiere Macmillan's *Romeo and Juliet* – says that Nureyev often found projects for her even when she was suffering from weight issues and depression and thus had trouble finding roles.

By the end of the 1970s, when he was in his 40s, he continued to tackle big classical roles. However by the late 1980s his diminished capabilities disappointed his admirers who had fond memories of his outstanding prowess and skill. His artistic directorship of the Paris Opera Ballet was a great success lifting the company out of a dark period. His *Sleeping Beauty* remains in the repertoire and was revived and filmed with his protégé Manuel Legris in the lead. When he was sick towards the end of his life, he worked on a final production of *La Bayadère* which closely follows the Kirov Ballet version he danced as a young man.

Personal life

Nureyev was homosexual, although he did have several heterosexual relationships as a younger man. Nureyev met Erik Bruhn, the celebrated Danish dancer, after Nureyev defected to the West in 1961. Nureyev was a great admirer of Bruhn, having seen filmed performances of the Dane on tour in Russia with the American Ballet Theatre, although stylistically the two dancers were very different. Bruhn and Nureyev became a couple and the two remained together off and on, with a very volatile relationship for 25 years, until Bruhn's death in 1986.

Final years

When AIDS appeared in France around 1982, Nureyev took little notice. The dancer tested positive for HIV in 1984, but for several years he simply denied that anything was wrong with his health. Nureyev began a marked decline only in the summer of 1991 and entered the final phase of the disease in the spring of 1992.

In March 1992, Rudolf Nureyev, living with advanced AIDS, visited Kazan and appeared as a conductor in front of the audience at Musa Cälil Tatar Academic Opera and Ballet Theater in Kazan, which now presents the Rudolf Nureyev Festival in Tatarstan Returning to Paris, with a high fever, he was admitted to the hospital Notre Dame du Perpétuel Secours in Levallois-Perret, a suburb northwest of Paris, and was operated on for pericarditis, an inflammation of the membranous sac around the heart. At that time, what inspired him to fight his illness was the hope that he could fulfill an invitation to conduct Prokofiev's *Romeo and Juliet* at an American Ballet Theater's benefit on 6 May 1992 at the Metropolitan Opera House in New York. He did so and was elated at the reception.

In July 1992, Nureyev showed renewed signs of pericarditis but determined to forswear further treatment. His last public appearance on 8 October 1992, at the premiere at Palais Garnier of a new production of *La Bayadère* that he choreographed after Marius Petipa for the Paris Opera Ballet. Nureyev had managed to obtain a photocopy of the original score by Minkus when in Russia in 1989. This meant that the full four acts of the ballet could be performed for the first time in the west since the Russian revolution. The ballet was a personal triumph although the gravity of his condition was evident. The French Culture Minister, Jack Lang, presented him that evening on stage with France's highest cultural award, the *Commandeur de l'Ordre des Arts et des Lettres*.

Death, funeral and tributes

Nureyev re-entered the hospital Notre Dame du Perpétuel Secours in Levallois-Perret on 20 November 1992 and remained there until his death from cardiac complication a few months later, aged 54. His funeral was held in the marble foyer of the Paris Garnier Opera House. Many paid tributes to his brilliance as a dancer. One such tribute

Nureyev's tomb in Sainte-Geneviève-des-Bois designed by Ezio Frigerio executed in mosaic by Akomena

came from Oleg Vinogradov of the Kirov Ballet in St. Petersburg, Russia, What Nureyev did in the west, he could have never have done here.

Nureyev's grave, at a Russian cemetery in Sainte-Geneviève-des-Bois near Paris, features a tomb draped in a mosaic of an oriental carpet. Nureyev was an avid collector of beautiful carpets and antique textiles. As his coffin was lowered into the ground, music from the last act of *Giselle* was played and his ballet shoes were cast into the grave along with white lilies.

After so many years of having been denied a place in the Kirov Ballet history, Nureyev's reputation was restored. His name was reentered in the history of the Kirov and some of his personal effects were placed on display at the theatre museum in St. Petersburg. At the famed Vaganova Academy a rehearsal room was named in his honour.

Influence

Nureyev's influence on the world of ballet changed the perception of male dancers; in his own productions of the classics the male roles received much more choreography. Another important influence was his crossing the borders between classical ballet and modern dance by performing both. Today it is normal for dancers to receive training in both styles, but Nureyev was the originator and excelled in modern and classical dance. He went out of his way to work with modern dance great, Martha Graham, and she created a work specially for him. While Gene Kelly had done much to combine modern and classical styles in film, he came from a more Modern Dance influenced "popular dance" environment, while Nureyev made great strides in gaining acceptance of Modern Dance in the "Classical Ballet" sphere.

Source http://en.wikipedia.org/wiki/Rudolf_Nureyev

Scott Ross (harpsichordist)

Scott Ross (March 1, 1951 – June 13, 1989) was a United States-born harpsichordist who lived in France for many years. His recordings include the first integral edition by a single performer of the 555 harpsichord sonatas of Domenico Scarlatti.

Biography

Scott 'Stonebreaker' Ross was born in Pittsburgh, Pennsylvania. He was nearly crippled by a severe scoliosis that kept him in a corset for much of his early life.

He studied piano and organ in Pittsburgh. Following the death of his father he moved to France with his mother in 1964, where he studied harpsichord at the Conservatoire de Nice. While living in Nice his mother committed suicide when Ross was aged 17. After completing his studies at Nice, he enrolled at the Conservatoire National Superieur in Paris.

In 1971 he was awarded the prestigious first prize of the "Concours de Bruges". Ross also took classes at the Royal Conservatory of Antwerp from Kenneth Gilbert.

He then began a teaching career at the School of Music, Université Laval, Quebec. While there, he made award-winning recordings of the complete *Pièces de Clavecin* by Rameau. Ross dressed in similar fashion to his students (even in performance), and his 'granny' spectacles appeared to align him more with the popular music icon John Lennon than the authentic performance scholar Gustav Leonhardt. For one concert at Université Laval that was attended by the university chancellor and the French Consul General he wore jeans and a red lumberjack shirt. Self-effacing to a fault, he explained, "I started the Goldbergs 'cause I quit smoking and, to keep one's fingers busy, it's better than knitting".

A passionate collector of orchids, his other hobbies included volcanology, mineralogy, and mycology. His keyboard interests were similarly wide ranging, extending beyond the harpsichord to the music of Frédéric Chopin, Claude Debussy and Maurice Ravel that he performed on the piano, and he also accompanied Schubert lieder. He loved the music of Brian Eno and Philip Glass, and was a fan of the punk performance artist Nina Hagen. Comparisons which might be drawn between Ross and the Canadian pianist Glenn Gould (e.g., due to their common love of Baroque music and their unconventional approaches) are put into a fuller context by these comments from Ross in a documentary film made toward the end of his life:

" When I hear nutcases like Glenn "
Gould who do: [plays staccato
version of J.S. Bach's Partita no.
1, BWV 825, *Allemande*], I say
he understood nothing of Bach's
music! I've listened carefully to
his records: he didn't understand. He was very brilliant; I re-
spect him up to a certain point.
For me, the fact that an artist
doesn't appear in public poses a
problem. But at least he was a
guy with the courage not to do
things like other people. All the
same, he was wide off the mark,
so wide off the mark that you'd
need a 747 to bring him back.
I'm hard on Glenn Gould. Well,
he's dead now, so I won't attack
a colleague.

In 1983 Ross took an indefinite sabbatical from Laval, embarking on a recording of François Couperin's *Suites pour le Clavecin*, as well as the music of other composers including Bach, George

Friderio Handel, Girolamo Frescobaldi and Jean-Henri d'Anglebert. He returned to his beloved France, renting a small house in Assas, near Montpellier, and another in Paris. In 1984 he signed a five-year recording-contract with Erato, but also experienced his first premonition of the illness that would later kill him.

The main fruit of his new contract was the daunting task of recording the complete keyboard sonatas (555 in total) of Domenico Scarlatti, a project started by Radio France, which decided to broadcast the sonatas in celebration of the 300th anniversary of the composer's birth, in 1985. Scott Ross began recording the sonatas on June 16, 1984, and during the eighteen months of recording he knew he had a fatal illness. Ninety-eight sessions were required, and the last take was completed on September 10, 1985. In all, there had been eight thousand takes. The recording was released on the Erato label as *Domenico Scarlatti, Complete Keyboard Works* in a set of 34 CDs.

Ross died of unattended pneumonia related to AIDS – he had no health insurance at that time – on June 13, 1989 in his house in Assas, France, aged 38.

Source http://en.wikipedia.org/wiki/Scott_Ross_(harpsichordist)

Serge Daney

Serge Daney (June 4, 1944, Paris – June 12, 1992) was an influential French movie critic who went on from writing film reviews to developing a "television criticism" and onto building a personal theory of the image. Although highly regarded in French and European film criticism circles, his work remains little known to English-speaking audiences, largely because it has not been consistently translated.

Biography

At the Voltaire High School in Paris, Daney received his first film teachings from Henri Agel, one of the most respected critics of the time. With two high school friends, Louis Skorecki and Claude Dépêche, he founded a short-lived film magazine called *Visages du cinéma* which only saw two editions, on Howard Hawks (containing Daney's first published text - a review of Rio Bravo called "An Adult Art") and on Otto Preminger.

In 1964, Daney joined the French film magazine *Cahiers du cinéma* with a series of interviews of American film directors (notably Howard Hawks, Leo McCarey, Josef von Sternberg and Jerry Lewis) conducted with Jean Louis Noames (aka Louis Skorecki) during a trip to Hollywood. He writes regularly for the magazine which was moving on from its "yellow cover" beginnings (the time of André Bazin, François Truffaut, Jean-Luc Godard, Éric Rohmer and Jacques Rivette - roughly 1951-1959) and was about to enter a period of heavy theoretical debates and radical political engagement after 1968.

Between 1968 and 1971, Daney also makes a series of travels to India, Morocco and Africa and starts lecturing cinema at the Censier University (Paris III). After *Cahiers*' failure to create a "Revolutionary Cultural Front", Daney took the responsibility of the magazine in 1973, supported by Serge Toubiana. Together, they operated a "return to cinema" for the magazine and also invited thinkers from outside the field of cinema: Michel Foucault, Jacques Rancière and Gilles Deleuze.

In 1981, Daney left *Cahiers* for the French daily newspaper *Libération*, to which he had contributed occasionally since its creation in 1973. Writing first about cinema, his focus turns more and more towards television. In 1987, for a hundred days, he wrote daily about French television in a column called "The wage of the channel hopper". From 1988 to 1991, he wrote a column on how films look when they are shown on television. He also wrote small pamphlets increasingly critical of television programs before he abandoned writing about television altogether in 1991, after a critical analysis of the television coverage of the Gulf War.

Daney went on to found the quarterly film magazine *Trafic* in which he wrote four pieces before dying of AIDS in June 1992.

Daney's general theory of the moving image became highly influential for the conception of 1997's documenta X, the tenth installment of the world's most important exhibition for contemporary art besides the Venice Biennale. The curator of documenta X, Catherine David, and her most important intellectual collaborator, Jean-François Chevrier, sought to integrate film and television into a show that was meant to deliver a critical investigation of the contemporary state of the image, and found in Daney's writings one of their guidelines.

Daney had other passions such as tennis and bullfights.

Source http://en.wikipedia.org/wiki/Serge_Daney

Severo Sarduy

Severo Sarduy (Camagüey, Cuba; February 25, 1937 – Paris; June 8, 1993) was a Cuban poet, author, playwright, and critic of Cuban literature and art.

Biography

Sarduy went to the equivalent of high school in Camagüey and in 1956 moved to Havana, where he began a study of medicine. With the triumph of the Cuban revolution he collaborated with the *Diario libre* and *Lunes de revolución*, pro-Marxist papers. In 1960 he traveled to Paris to study at the Ecole du Louvre. There he was connected to the group of intellectuals who produced the magazine *Tel Quel*, particularly to philosopher François Wahl, with whom he was openly involved. Sarduy worked as a reader for *Editions du Seuil* and as editor and producer of the *Radiodiffusion-Télévision Française*. In 1972 his novel *Cobra* won him the Medici Prize. He was among the most brilliant essayists writing in Spanish and "a powerful baroque narrator, full of surprising resources.". As a poet, he was considered one of the greatest of his time. He was also a more or less secret painter; a major retrospective of his work was held at the Reina Sofía Museum of Madrid after his death. He died due to complications from AIDS just after finishing his autobiographical work *Los pájaros de la playa*.

Along with Alejo Carpentier, José Lezama Lima, Virgilio Piñera, and Reinaldo Arenas, Sarduy is one of the most famous Cuban writers of the twentieth century; some of his works deal explicitly with male homosexuality and transvestism.

Source http://en.wikipedia.org/wiki/Severo_Sarduy

Thierry Le Luron

French DVD cover for a Thierry Le Luron compilation.

Thierry Le Luron (French pronunciation: [tjɛ.ʁi.lə.ly'ʁɔ̃] ; 2 April 1952 – 13 November 1986) was a French impersonator and humorist.

Debut

At the age of 17 years, Thierry Le Luron, student at the Lycée Emmanuel Mounier in Chatenay-Malabry, creates a band with friends (The dead rats) and a few scenes in the Hauts-de-Seine and around a . It debuted in several Parisian cabarets, including Jacob's Ladder, in 1969 . The public first met him on 4 January 1970 at the Game of chance, a sequence of the television broadcast TV Sunday he won six consecutive times, singing tunes rather classic before choosing to devote themselves to imitation. He performed his first sketches in the same issue, including the 1 st February 1970 (imitation Adamo) or the 15 February 1970, the anniversary of Jean Nohain where it simulates Jacques Chaban-Delmas and Jean Nohain . In 1971, he released his first album The Ministry woozy, which is very popular. He gave his first performance as a star at Bobino in February–March 1972 and is the first part of Claude François on tour in the summer of 1972.

Success

From November 1972 to July 1973, he hosted his first show on the first French channel : The Tomboy Sunday . It creates the same year his new show at the Variety Theatre .

Thierry Le Luron tests each evening with his friends his last portraits fierce. The "band The Tomboy" includes Jacques Collard, Jacques Pessis, Pierre Guillermo, Francis Diwo Fournol and Luke and Bernard Mabille . In joyful feast in the restaurant of The Chamarré Jacques Collard, then at the Alcazar of Jean Marie River, and finally Castel, portraits, sketches and imitations are refined and give birth to very elaborate performances: the Olympia (December 1976), Bobino (February- April 1978), Theatre Marigny (October 1979-June 1980), Thierry Extravaganza at the Palais des Congress in Paris (November 1980-January 1981), From de Gaulle to Mitterrand at the Marigny Theatre (January- December 1983), The Tomboy released at the theater Gymnasium Mary Bell (November 1984-March 1986).

The last show attracted 400,000 viewers 2 . He then worked mainly with Bernard Mabille and created the character of Adolf Benito glandular, concierge rue de Bievre 3, "fairly extensive caricature of the average French: an individual with no particular creed, influenced by events, and that defines the Tomboy: Pétain under Vichy, under General de Gaulle and Socialist May 10 to 11! " 2 .

It runs parallel to an intense television and radio: Chat pocket of Georges Feydeau as part of the theater tonight (released 24 October 1975), a number of Maritie and Gilbert Carpentier (March 1976 and June 1979) This is the show (1,980 - 1981), etc.. From 1978 to 1979, he hosted a weekly show, The Parasites of the antenna, on France Inter including Deerhunter, Lawrence Riesner, Bernard Mabille and Evelyne Grandjean as columnists. In 1981, he recorded the credits of the animated television series Rody little Cid 4 .

Known for his impersonations of Valery Giscard d'Estaing when he was president (1974-1981), Thierry Le Luron Live parody Gilbert Bécaud, when issuing the Champs Elysees of 10 November 1984, singing and blackmailing the public 's annoying, it's the rose - the rose being the symbol of the Socialist Party, in power since 1981, he dedicated this song to President Francois Mitterrand 5 .

On 25 September 1985, he "married for better or for laughter" with great fanfare a Coluche disguised as a bride, a parody of marriage to Yves Mourousi to be held three days later at Nîmes . The Tomboy said: "the future Mrs. Mourousi is sure to have both ears" 6 . This statement and the false marriage itself are often interpreted as a spike to a wedding and Yves Mourousi suspected lip, the latter being rather experienced in all of Paris at least, to his adventures male 7.

Source http://en.wikipedia.org/wiki/Thierry_Le_Luron

Thierry Paulin

Thierry Paulin (November 28, 1963 – April 16, 1989) was a French serial killer active in the 1980s.

Thierry Paulin
Background information

Also known as	The Monster of Montmartre, The Beast of Montmartre The Old Lady Killer
Born	November 28, 1963 Fort-de-France, Martinique
Died	April 16, 1989 (aged 25) Fresnes Prison, Fresnes, France
Cause of death	AIDS
Conviction	Died before trial
Killings	
Number of victims	18+
Country	France
Date apprehended	1987

Childhood and teenage years

Paulin was born in Fort-de-France, Martinique. His father flew to France just after his birth, leaving his teen-aged mother to fend for herself and the baby. Paulin was raised in Martinique by his paternal grandmother, who owned a restaurant and allegedly paid little attention to her grandson. When he was ten, Paulin started to live with his now married mother, trying to blend in with his stepbrothers and sisters. His behavior started to become erratic and violent towards the other children, and eventually his mother asked his father to take their son to France. His father accepted in order to avoid paying alimony.

As a mixed-race student among white peers, Paulin had few friends, and performed poorly at school, failing his exams. At the age of 17, he decided to enter military service early, joining the parachutists' troops; however, his fellow soldiers disdained him for his race and homosexuality.

On November 14, 1982, he robbed an old woman in her grocery, menacing her with a knife; the grocer knew him as a client, however, and he was soon arrested. In June 1983, he was sentenced to two years of jail, but the sentence was suspended ("avec sursis"), allowing Paulin to remain free.

From Toulouse to Paris

In 1984, after leaving the army, Paulin learned that his mother and her family now lived in Nanterre, a northern suburb of Paris. He went there to live with them, but his relationship was hostile.

Paulin became a waiter at the Paradis Latin, a night-club renowned for its transvestite shows. There, he started a career as an artist, dressed in drag and singing tunes by his favourite singer, Eartha Kitt. His mother was once invited to watch her son's performance, but she left the club a few seconds after the beginning of the act.

The most important event that happened to Paulin at the Paradis Latin was meeting Jean-Thierry Mathurin. The 19-year-old Mathurin was born in French Guyana, and was a drug addict. Paulin fell in love with him and they soon became lovers. Paulin was also addicted, but less severely, and sold drugs as well.

On October 5, 1984, two elderly women were assaulted in Paris. Germaine Petitot, 91, survived but was too traumatized to give a detailed description of the criminals. Anna Barbier-Ponthus, 83, died after being beaten and asphyxiated beneath a pillow. Her murderer robbed her of 300 francs (about $50).

In October-November 1984, eight other old women were murdered, mainly in the 18th precinct of Paris, but in neighboring precincts too. The violence of the crimes was horrific; some of the victims had their heads stuck into plastic bags, some were beaten to death, and one of them was forced to drink drain cleaner. In all cases, the motive appeared to be robbery. Some reports allege that Paulin singled out women who seemed unpleasant or unfriendly when he engaged them in conversation, while Paulin himself told police that "I only tackled the weakest of them."

At the same time, Paulin and Mathurin were leading an extravagant lifestyle, spending their nights dancing, drinking champagne, and snorting cocaine. In late November, they decided to go to Toulouse to stay for a few months at the home of Paulin's father. But the elder Paulin was unable to accept his son's lover, and violent fights ensued, ending when Paulin and Mathurin broke up. Mathurin returned to Paris, while Paulin tried to start his own firm of transvestite artists, a plan which failed in autumn 1985.

The second wave of murders

From December 20, 1985, to June 14, 1986, eight more old women were murdered. The police were unable to identify the killer, though the investigators had a few clues. Police determined through fingerprint evidence that the perpetrator was the same individual who committed the 1984 murders. However, in the new murders, the killer appeared to favor quicker, less cruel methods.

In the autumn of 1986, Paulin attacked one of his cocaine dealers with a baseball bat. The dealer went to the police, and Paulin was arrested. Paulin was sentenced to 16 months of jail for the assault, spending one year in Fresnes prison. Upon his release, Paulin knew himself to be HIV-positive.

The final countdown

Knowing that he was in effect under a death sentence from AIDS, Paulin organized lavish parties, spending a lot of money and sparing no expense. Paulin paid for these parties with stolen credit cards and checks, and with the proceeds from his murders.

On November 25, 1987, Paulin murdered Rachel Cohen, age 79. On the same day, he attacked an 87-year-old woman, Berthe Finalteri, whom he suffocated and left for dead. Two days later, he strangled Genevieve Germont, who would be his last victim.

As Paulin celebrated his 24th birthday, Madame Finalteri unexpectedly recovered, and was able to give an accurate description of her attacker, stating that he was *"un métis d'une vingtaine d'année coiffée à la Carl Lewis, avec une boucle d'oreille gauche"* (literally "a mix-race man in his twenties, with hair like Carl Lewis and an earring in his left ear"). On December 1, Paulin was arrested while walking down the street when a local police inspector, Francis Jacob, recognized him from Madame Finalteri's description. After two days in custody, Paulin admitted everything, including his involvement with Mathurin. Accused of committing 18 murders (though he claimed responsibility for 21), he was sent to jail awaiting trial.

In early 1988, Paulin fell ill, as his body began to succumb to the effects of AIDS. Within a year he was hospitalized in a state of near-paralysis, suffering from both tuberculosis and meningitis. He died during the night of April 16, 1989, in the hospital wing of Fresnes prison.

Only Mathurin was tried for the first nine attacks and murders, receiving a life sentence, plus 18 years without parole. He was incarcerated until January 2009, while technically, Thierry Paulin was never convicted of the murders of which he was accused.

Film references

The 1994 movie *J'ai pas sommeil* (*I Can't Sleep*), by director Claire Denis (*Chocolat*, *No Fear No Die*) was based on the Paulin case.

Source http://en.wikipedia.org/wiki/Thierry_Paulin

Vincent Fourcade

Portrait of Vincent Fourcade

Vincent Gabriel Fourcade (27 February 1934 – 23 December 1992) was a French interior designer and the business and life partner of Robert Denning. "Outrageous luxury is what our clients want," he once said.

Family and youth

"Born...to a family of distinguished French aesthetes, the designer spent many of his formative years in a twenty-bedroom house replete with made-to-order Majorelle furnishings." "I learned my trade by going out every evening as a young man," he told art historian Rosamond Bernier. "I went to every pretty house in France and Italy and other places too, and I remembered them all, even down to what was on each little table." Vincent was educated at University College London.

New York City

A handsome eligible bachelor, he was never without invitations in the United States either. He tried a career in banking, the business of his father and grandfather in Paris. He met Robert Denning in 1959. Denning a *protégé* of Edgar de Evia, had acquired an eye for design and effect from working with the photographer on sets for many fabric and furniture accounts, and with whom he shared one of the most magnificent Manhattan apartments on the top three floors of the Rhinelander Mansion. It would be here that early clients such as Lillian Bostwick Phipps and her husband Ogden Phipps would be entertained as de Evia was spending more and more time on his estate in Greenwich, Connecticut. While Vincent would take Ogden Phipps to good dealers where he would spend millions of dollars on signed pieces of French furniture, Bob would take Lillian Bostwick Phipps down to 11th Street. "It infuriated Vincent. He used to say 'Bobby, you have ruined the Phippses for me by giving Mrs. Phipps that strange appetite for 11th Street.'"

Robert Denning sitting in front of a portrait of Vincent Fourcade

Denning & Fourcade

Slowly the pair became known for an extreme of luxury compared to le goût Rothschild. An early party that they styled included covering the floor with a hundred old raccoon coats. In 1960 they formed the firm of Denning & Fourcade, Inc. which would for over forty-five years set a standard for a list of

clients that read like a social registry. Referred to in *New York* magazine as "...the Odd Couple. Boyish, down-to-earth Denning is the hardest worker, while Fourcade sniffs the client air to gauge if it's socially registered before he goes beyond the fringe." Early clients included old friends that he had known socially such as Michel David-Weill. Jackie Kennedy met his mark and two of her notes to him survive, the first thanking him for his letter after the assassination of her brother-in-law Robert F. Kennedy, with the cancellation over her signature since as the widow of a president of the United States she still had franking privileges. She lost this when she remarried. The other, a handwritten note postmarked 28 October 1976 over a thirteen cent stamp —
Dear Vincent, I have never eaten such delicious food in such incredibly beautiful surroundings in my life. Thank you so <u>very very</u> much. affectionately Jackie.
The return address also handwritten – Onassis, 1040 5th Ave.

Homes

Living with AIDS

Early in the 1980s Fourcade contracted AIDS. He kept his looks and strength through most of that decade as Denning and he would divide their time between New York and Paris, crossing the Atlantic on the Concorde. His older brother Xavier Fourcade, the internationally known contemporary art dealer, died of the disease in 1987 at St. Luke's-Roosevelt Hospital Center in New York City.

By 1990 the disease would take control his life and early in 1992 Denning & Fourcade would with a nurse take the Concorde one last time to Paris where he would live his remaining days in their apartment at 16 rue de Chazelles, just up the street from the studio of the sculptor Frédéric Bartholdi who is best known for the Statue of Liberty.
Source http://en.wikipedia.org/wiki/Vincent_Fourcade

Yves Mourousi

Yves Mourousi, 1985.

Yves Mourousi (20 July 1942, Suresnes, Hauts-de-Seine - 7 April 1998, Paris) was a French television and radio news presenter and journalist. He was the TF1 midday news ("journal de 13h00") anchor during 14 years between 1975 to 1988 and one of the most popular TV presenter at this time.

His name, Mourousi come from his mother, a Russian princess of Phanariote nobility.

During the 1980s, he is a member of a French Press organization for Musichall, Circus, Dance and Arts presided by a well known journalist in France, Jacqueline Cartier, with authors or notable personalities as Pierre Cardin, Guy des Cars, Francis Fehr and Jean-Pierre Thiollet.

Source http://en.wikipedia.org/wiki/Yves_Mourousi

Yves Rault

Yves Rault
Born 1 August 1958
Died 16 September 1997 (aged 39)
Occupation pianist
Years active 1980-unknown

Yves Rault (1 August 1958 – 16 September 1997) was a French pianist. He started to play the piano at age of six. From 1968 he lived in Saint-Jean-de-Luz where he studied with Ada Labeque until he entered the Conservatoire National Superieur de Musique de Paris: he completed his musical studies at the age of 17 winning a 1st Piano Prize (class of Yvonne Loriod) and a 1st Prize in Chamber Music (class of Geneviève Joy). Subsequently, he attended the master-classes of eminent musicians such as Vlado Perlemuter, Nikita Magaloff, Rafael Da Silva, Charles Rosen, György Sebök, Paul Badura-Skoda and Claude Helffer.

Awarded a Fulbright Scholarship in 1979, he decided to perfect his skills in New York studying at the Juilliard School with Jacob Lateiner and William Masselos: in the meanwhile, he obtained the 1st Prize at the Gina Bachauer International Piano Competition. He also won several other International Piano Competitions (Maria Canals International Music Competition 2nd Prize in Barcelona, Marsala's 2nd Prize, Vercelli's 4th Prize, Epinal's 4th Prize...). A dazzling career starts with new international awards: Grand Prize of the Charles Cros Academy with the violinist Raphael Oleg for their recording of Schumann's Sonatas (1980), 3rd Prize and Special Prize of Contemporary Music at the Paloma O'Shea International Piano Competition in Santander (1982), 1st Prize at the Ciudade do Porto International Piano Competition (1984).

These successes led him to give recitals around the world: France, Spain, Holland, Italy, Portugal, Switzerland, United States, Japan, Australia and South Africa. He performed regularly with various orchestras (Radio France New Philharmonic Orchestra, Spanish Radio Television Orchestra, Orchestre national du Capitole de Toulouse...). He was invited as a soloist by various foreign televisions and radios, and has also recorded for Radio France and French Television.

The eclecticism of his tastes led him to become interested in a diverse and sometimes unexplored repertoire (Ricardo Viñes, Ernesto Nazareth, Guillaume Lekeu...) and his interest for the contemporary music made him participate in many first performances mainly with the Montpellier Philharmonic Orchestra and with several French contemporary musical ensembles such as 2E2M, GERM, Musique Oblique, and Contrechamps.

Rault died in Paris of AIDS on 16 September 1997, at the age of 39.

Source http://en.wikipedia.org/wiki/Yves_Rault